W9-DED-091

GEONOMICS INSTITUTE FOR INTERNATIONAL ECONOMIC
ADVANCEMENT SERIES
Michael P. Claudon, Series Editor

Comrades Go Private

Strategies for Eastern European Privatization

Edited by Michael P. Claudon
and Tamar L. Gutner

NEW YORK UNIVERSITY PRESS
New York and London

HC
244
C59
1992

© 1992 by Geonomics Institute for International Economic Advancement
All rights reserved
Manufactured in the United States of America

Library of Congress Cataloging-in-Publication Data

Comrades go private : strategies for Eastern European privatization /
edited by Michael P. Claudon and Tamar L. Gutner.
    p.   cm. — (Geonomics Institute for International Economic
Advancement series)
  Based on papers presented at a seminar, held Sept. 1990 by the
Geonomics Institute for International Economic Advancement.
  Includes index.
  ISBN 0-8147-1459-5 (cloth)
  1. Europe, Eastern—Economic policy—Congresses.   2. Europe, Eastern—
Economic conditions—1989—Congresses.   3. Privatization—Europe, Eastern—
Congresses.   4. Germany—History—Unification, 1990—Congresses.
I. Claudon, Michael P.   II. Gutner, Tamar L.   III. Geonomics Institute for
International Economic Advancement.   IV. Series.
HC244.C59   1992
338.947—dc20   91-28968
                                                          CIP

FLORIDA STATE
UNIVERSITY LIBRARIES

OCT 9 1992

TALLAHASSEE, FLORIDA

New York University Press books are printed on acid-free paper,
and their binding materials are chosen for strength and durability.

Contents

Acknowledgments

Many have contributed to the success of this East-West venture. In the first place, this volume has benefited from the generosity of the conference sponsors: The Dun & Bradstreet Corporation; Edward Aycoth & Company, Inc.; Henry Kaufman & Company, Inc.; Heytesbury Inc.; The International Bank Credit Analyst; Jones International, Inc.; MMS International, Inc.; New York Stock Exchange, Inc.; Scott-European Corporation; and Sharpoint. The conference also benefited from the participation of a large and diverse group of specialists on East-West relations, the names and affiliations of whom are listed at the end of this volume.

The staff of the Geonomics Institute, including Nancy Ward, Elizabeth Leeds, George Bellerose, and Elizabeth Cleary, ably assisted in organizing and executing many aspects of the conference program. Colleen Duncan provided editorial assistance and shepherded the preparations of the volume for publication from the conference through several stages of revisions, to this updated final version. Their contributions were invaluable.

The Editors

Foreword

Poland, Hungary, and Czechoslovakia have resolutely led Eastern Europe into uncharted space. Defining the goals of economic reform is trivial compared to determining how best to wean these former command economies from artificially cheap supplies of Soviet energy and raw materials and transform them into lean, internationally competitive market-based societies.

The big three Eastern European economies have plunged ahead and collectively submitted to shock therapy. Through a sometimes chaotic process of spontaneous and state-directed privatization, a private sector of cooperatives and private enterprises, joint ventures, and foreign enterprises is literally exploding on the scene. Imperative planning and physical targets for enterprises and ministries, and bureaucratically selected and administered prices, are being replaced by purely indicative macroeconomic targets.

Along with privatization of state assets and massive market reforms have come massive unemployment rates, bankrupt enterprises, near hyperinflation, and an accelerating economic slowdown.

In addition to comprehensive political reform, the countries of Eastern Europe must simultaneously grapple with three daunting economic and political tasks: domestic and foreign macroeconomic stabilization, institution-building and sectoral restructuring, and the transition from central planning to a market-based economy.

Both inflation and repressed inflation (shortages) must be eliminated. External stabilization entails building net export flows to levels capable of servicing the imprudent external debt loads that have destroyed or severely threatened their creditworthiness.

Institution-building must also receive national attention and resources. Laws are being written and enacted but not enforced. Separation of central banking and commercial banking is a must, followed by establishing institutions to oversee and foster the development of a competitive commercial banking industry. Financial markets and stock markets must be established to facilitate financial intermediation. Spontaneous privatization must be replaced by a rational equitable process.

The seminar from which this volume derives was sponsored by the Geonomics Institute in September 1990. The resulting volume focuses on issues related to privatization. In addition to dealing with the reform process, two central questions are addressed: To what extent, if at all, does German reunification offer a privatization model for the remainder of Eastern Europe? And why have Poland and Hungary, and to a lesser extent Czechoslovakia, chosen speed over concerns about social justice in the privatization process?

Geonomics' mission is to seek solutions to global economic and business problems. Consistent with its mission to find solutions, not just contemplate them, Geonomics is now creating and acting as a catalyst for implementing realistic and feasible solutions to problems related to Soviet and Eastern European business law and financial institution reform, one of the great challenges for the remainder of the twentieth century.

Geonomics seminars bring together small groups of business leaders, policymakers, and scholars to identify and analyze key issues. In subsequent workshops multilateral working groups develop detailed policy recommendations or draft legislation. Finally, the Geonomics Institute is the catalyst for developing self-sustaining programs that address and correct specific economic problems.

We welcome comments, reactions, and questions regarding the Geonomics Institute and its programs.

Michael P. Claudon
President and Managing Director
Geonomics Institute

Introduction

Once Eastern Europe's communist regimes relinquished their hold on power, the region's new governments began the daunting task of transforming centralized economies into market economies based on private ownership. They may share similar goals, but there is little consensus on how to achieve them. Indeed, the countries most explicitly embarking on radical reform—Hungary, Czechoslovakia and Poland—are each developing their own reform strategy, based on different domestic political and economic contexts.

The Solidarity-led government in Poland, for example, opted for "shock therapy," as the best way to tackle hyperinflation and to shorten the difficult transition period that lay ahead. The Hungarian government, by contrast, with a healthier economy and much more experience with reform, could afford to adopt what is described in Catherine M. Sokil's paper as a "consensus program" that emphasizes gradual liberalization. Czechoslovakia's leaders, constrained by the ongoing debate pitting those in favor of rapid change against those opting for a gradual shift, seem to prefer a route somewhere between those of its neighbors. In all cases, policymakers must contend with a formidable array of obstacles, ranging from an antiquated or underdeveloped industrial infrastructure and distorted ownership structures to declining economic growth. At the same time, they are moving through a political minefield, because public expectations are high and disillusionment is spreading. There is a groundswell for fast reform, yet re-

1

form's painful side effects—sharp price increases, rising unemployment, and plummeting output, for example—can erode popular support.

Privatization is a key feature of the reform plans. Although the 1980s was a decade of privatization for scores of countries, past experiences may offer few, if any, lessons for Eastern Europe. Indeed, the scale and speed of denationalization planned in this region is unprecedented. Never before have countries attempted to shift virtually their entire economy from public to private hands. In Poland, for example, more than 90 percent of production is in state hands, and the government hopes to sell around 7,000 enterprises, producing more than half the country's gross domestic product, over the next few years. Hungary and Czechoslovakia have similar goals. By contrast, Robert L. Konski and Andrew G. Berg point out that between 1980 and 1987, the busiest years in what they call the Decade of Privatization, only six hundred firms throughout the world left state hands. Moreover, privatization in Eastern Europe means much more than the transfer of ownership; it is seen as a key ingredient in creating a new economic system, a market economy, and a pluralist democracy. Privatization policies will play a crucial role in shaping not just the new economies but the new politics of Eastern Europe.

Privatization is often hailed as a panacea. It is expected to raise money for the government budget; stimulate economic growth; attract foreign capital, technology and management; legitimate new or young stock and capital markets; and integrate the economy into the world system. It is also seen as a tool to strengthen and widen political support for new governments. Following former British Prime Minister Margaret Thatcher's privatization strategy, all three governments are keen to spread share ownership as widely as possible among the domestic population. Consequently, employee stock ownership plans and other forms of leveraged buyouts that would concentrate ownership in a smaller group of hands, while popular among many Western observers, have not received an enthusiastic reception in Eastern Europe.

Despite their high hopes, an increasing number of government officials realize their expectations are inflated as the costs associated with different privatization strategies become apparent. Privatization will produce winners and losers by shifting power and/or

creating new relationships within and among the broad categories of labor, management, shareholders, and the general
population. In all three countries, people are worried that privatization will benefit some workers, while forcing others into the
ranks of the unemployed, as redundant jobs are cut or enterprises
go bankrupt. People are also concerned about foreign domination
of key industries and corruption that benefits players from the old
regimes. At the time of writing, Poland's privatization legislation, for example, limits foreign share ownership to 10 percent
without special permission. The first stage of Czechoslovakia's state
property auction, in January 1991, was only open to domestic citizens. In Hungary spontaneous privatization met with loud protest
that enterprise managers were selling state-owned enterprises to
themselves and their friends at bargain-basement prices.

The issue of speed or efficiency versus equity has dominated discussion in all three countries. Speedy privatization raises public
concern that a few (former elites) will benefit unduly at the expense of society, and/or that foreign investors will come in and
gobble up prize enterprises. The gradual approach, in turn, is criticized as only a "half reform," which could not only delay the necessary break between command economy and free market but also
leave economies in even worse shape. In addition, there are many
other disputes: Should the privatization process itself be privatized
and spontaneous, or should it be conducted by a government agency? Should foreign investment be restricted or encouraged? How
should a state enterprise be valued? At what price should enterprises be privatized? Which companies should be allowed to go
bankrupt? Should former owners have the right to reclaim their
property? Which enterprises should be privatized? At this stage,
questions like these far outnumber answers.

The Geonomics Institute brought together a group of economists,
policymakers, lawyers, business representatives, and consultants,
from East and West, to examine the impact of economic reform,
privatization, and German unification on a region in flux. At the
time of the seminar, the former German Democratic Republic
(GDR) and the Federal Republic of Germany (FRG) were not yet
unified. What one now calls awkwardly "eastern Germany" has
many of the same problems of transition as its neighbors to the
east, although its situation is unique. The former GDR began this

decade as part of an enlarged Germany, with a hard currency and
a sure and deep source of financial help. The papers produced at
the seminar focused on current debates about reform, and they provide a foundation for assessing the challenge the region presents to
the international system.

Chapters 1, 2, and 3 focus on the economic reform process evolving in Czechoslovakia, Hungary, and Poland, and the role of privatization in this process. Kalman Mizsei presents an overview of the
policy options facing the three countries. He describes their different economic starting points and shows how these as well as domestic political pressures shape the privatization policies being
adopted. Common to all countries in the region, Mizsei argues, is
the likelihood new political elites will shy away from policies that
might risk votes, in spite of the fact that the economic rationale for
privatization remains strong.

In Chapter 2 Catherine M. Sokil focuses on the case of Hungary,
which, she notes, has had a head start relative to its Eastern
European neighbors in reforming its economy and attracting
Western capital. She examines Hungary's centrally planned system and why it left the economy weak before addressing the evolution of the reform process. Looking ahead, Sokil argues that economics have been placed on the "back burner" while the country
adjusts itself to a new political climate. She describes the privatization policies put forward by the Blue Ribbon Commission, a multilateral group of analysts organized to advise the new government,
which recommends the privatization of most small firms within a
year, and the provision of special lines of credit to the public to help
people buy shares in privatized enterprises. Sokil predicts the
Commission's recommendations will be adopted, but she cautions
that the privatization process will be slow amid the skepticism of a
newly vocal population.

Chapters 3 and 4 analyze Poland's pioneering "shock-therapy"
stabilization program, which may serve as a model for other countries. Gregory Jedrzejczak argues in Chapter 3 that the radical nature of the government's stabilization program—which included a
sharp currency devaluation, price increases, and tight monetary
and fiscal measures—was necessary to choke hyperinflation and to
create the legal, institutional and economic foundation for a market economy. However, he admits that the impact of the stabiliza-

tion plan on domestic politics is not yet clear; on one hand the plan succeeded in reducing inflation and stabilizing the zloty, but at the same time unemployment increased sharply as industrial output plummeted. Privatization, he argues, will play a critical role in transforming the economy, both as a stimulus to growth and as a means of creating functioning capital markets.

Robert L. Konski and Andrew G. Berg add in Chapter 4 that privatization will have other positive impacts on the Polish economy, from creating opportunities for foreign investment that will bring to Poland technology and managerial skills to helping reduce the social costs of economic transformation. However, they point out that the process faces myriad obstacles, from a lack of local capital to the absence of an adequate financial and organizational infrastructure. Konski and Berg argue in favor of a rapid privatization process that is socially acceptable in the sense that it is broadly based and creates a new class of owners.

The case of Czechoslovakia is addressed in chapters 5 and 6 by Michal Mejstrik and Oldrich Dedek. Mejstrik argues in Chapter 5 that privatization must be accompanied by a break up of monopolies and steps to encourage competition in order to ensure the dissolution of collusive relationships between interest groups associated with monopolies and oligopolies. He points out that the government is already taking important steps toward building a market environment by implementing laws that make explicit a separation of the state's political and economic power as well as public and private law, while liberalizing prices and preparing for a convertible currency. Mejstrik describes the government plans for privatization, which will initially focus on light industry, and says that the government's intention to distribute equity to domestic citizens in the form of "vouchers" will deprive the treasury of sorely needed funds. He argues that a combination of leveraged buyouts and foreign capital can help tackle the problem of insufficient public savings while bringing in foreign know-how and giving employees incentives to support the reform effort.

Dedek analyzes in Chapter 6 the positive and negative impact of a reunited Germany on Czechoslovakia. Czechoslovakia will benefit from the economic growth in Germany fueled by unification and the injection of funds into the former GDR. He argues, however, that unification will hurt some of Czechoslovakia's economic sectors, particularly in consumer goods, as demand from eastern Germany shifts to higher-quality domestic production. Dedek believes the lessons Czechoslovakia can learn from eastern Germany's radical shift to a market economy are limited; eastern Germany's case is unique because the infusion of western German capital will soften the negative side effects of rapid change, such as unemployment. Radical reform, asserts Dedek, may be unwise in Czechoslovakia given the poor initial economic conditions. He advocates a more gradual transition and criticizes those "liberals" that opt for rapid change for neglecting to factor in the high social costs associated with radical restructuring.

Chapters 7, 8, and 9 redirect attention to a unified Germany and highlight its impact on Eastern European reform. Jenik Radon argues in Chapter 7 that Germany will be the locomotive of privatization in Eastern Europe because of its strong economy and geographical proximity to and trade ties with Eastern Europe. He believes the western German economy will also provide a model for Eastern European countries to follow. Radon maintains that the relatively unique structure of the German economy explains its strength. At its heart is the mid-sized firms, or *mittelstand*, which are characterized by flexible, hands-on management, an emphasis on constant improvement of its products, and a team-work approach. He feels the *mittelstand*, in setting up joint ventures in Eastern Europe, will encourage the growth of similar-sized firms in the region. Radon concludes that the German firms will be the main conduit for the transfer of Western business practices to Eastern Europe, while holding their positions as the leading foreign investors. He thinks the United States, in particular, is in danger of missing opportunities for investing in and having an impact on privatization in Eastern Europe.

In Chapter 8, David B. Audretsch and Heather Wayland warn that the economic transformation of the former East Germany is no easy task, despite comparative advantages. They review eastern Germany's structural deficiencies and examine the pros and cons of investment in eastern Germany. The authors conclude that the successful integration of eastern Germany in the west will depend on massive deregulation, the break up and privatization of the large monopolies, and the encouragement of free competition.

In Chapter 9, David P. Ellerman, Ales Vahcic, and Tea Petrin argue that "active ownership" is missing from the debates over privatization models and advocate privatization through manager/worker leveraged buyouts. Other methods, they say, are less efficient, because they ultimately dissipate ownership over a broad group of passive shareholders. The authors advocate a decentralized privatization process that allows for "spontaneous" privatizations within rules set by the government and enforced by a regulatory agency.

Together these papers provide a body of fresh, highly accessible but intellectually rigorous analysis from a multilateral cross-section of scholars, business people, and government officials. As such, this volume provides multidimensional insights into, and perspectives on, the challenges faced by these former Warsaw Pact nations as they tackle economic and political transformation.

This volume ends with the recommendations of the three seminar working groups. Among the conclusions is strong support for a pragmatic approach toward privatization that employs a variety of methods backed by strong legal and regulatory frameworks. In the speed versus equity debate, the participants took the position that rapid implementation of reform policies is essential. The cold shower of reform must be as abrupt as is institutionally and politically possible in order to shorten the already difficult transition period and avoid depressing these countries' economies even further.

Michael P. Claudon
Tamar L. Gutner

Part I

Strategies for
Eastern European Privatization

1

The Challenge of Privatization in East Central Europe

Kalman Mizsei

THE MACROECONOMIC AND SOCIAL FRAMEWORK

Privatization has been a popular macroeconomic policy device throughout the world since the early 1980s, but the lessons learned by both developed and less developed countries (LDCs) will not be easily applicable to Eastern Europe. Indeed, there are vast differences in the economic and political contexts between Eastern Europe and other nations that chose privatization.

In Eastern Europe virtually all productive assets have been in state hands for the last four decades. In contrast, an average of only 11–12 percent of assets are under state control in LDCs. There are only a few special cases (Argentina, Sri Lanka, and the Philippines, for example) in which most public assets are administered by the state. But even these special cases differ from Eastern Europe, which is emerging from a long period of brutal discrimination against private enterprise, individual profit maximization, and other characteristics of a market society.

One major consequence of omnipresent and oppressive state control is that privatization in Eastern Europe is being launched against a backdrop of inefficient, poorly managed state enterprise. In addition, Eastern Europe lacks the basic cultural values of a market society. Privatization has become a key policy objective in the region because it is seen as a means of correcting economic inefficiency, erasing shortages and inflationary pressures, and spurring greater worker productivity.

11

The Collapse of Rules of Conduct

By the beginning of the 1980s, Eastern European economies were suffering a fundamental "systemic" crisis that was both economic and, more importantly, institutional. Institutional crisis was especially severe in state firms. The legitimacy of state ownership, once the cornerstone of socialism, was seriously undermined. Due to the absence of clear rules for transforming public property to private property, stealing became a major means of acquiring property and/or wealth. This seriously undermined the creation of business ethics, fundamental to a viable capitalist society.

External Debt

In the latest period of communism, most regimes have prolonged their existence with funds raised by accumulating international debt. This is the single major reason for acute financial imbalances, even in cases such as Hungary, where there has been a marked improvement of macroeconomic management.

On the other hand, not all Eastern European countries face a critical debt burden. Czechoslovakia, for instance, followed a rather prudent borrowing policy in the last two decades; Romania repaid—at tremendous domestic, economic, and social costs—its debts in the 1980s; Albania, in turn, did not even allow indebtedness to occur. Finally, German reunification rendered the accumulated debt of the former German Democratic Republic unimportant. Poland, Yugoslavia, Hungary, Bulgaria, and, increasingly, the Soviet Union are in a debt trap, where even continuous and significant current-account surpluses cannot stop the growth of the debt overhang. International creditors would find it costly to write off Eastern European debt; indeed, just setting a possible example for the much more deeply indebted Latin America would be unacceptable. Eastern European countries' differing macroeconomic circumstances seriously impact the privatization policies that can be implemented. The more indebted countries can hardly avoid different kinds of declared or hidden trade-offs between their external and internal debts versus state equities. It means more willingness to sell, rather than freely distribute, state assets as well as more readiness to liberalize government regulations of foreign direct investment.

The legalization of the shadow private sector has already occurred in several Eastern European countries. The shadow economy flourished throughout the region, despite the fact that individualism was relegated to the hidden sphere of social life. A major difference occurred, however, in the attitudes of the political elite toward illegal economic activity. Hungary tried to incorporate private interests into the legal economy through its 1968 reform and liberalization of the small enterprise sphere in the 1980s. Poland opened the doors for major private arbitrage activity between the domestic and international economy as a result of its financial difficulties in the mid-1970s. Yugoslavia was able to let its citizens enter the European labor markets back in the 1960s, and it later opened its tourist sector to private investment. In contrast, the private sector was explicitly repressed in Czechoslovakia, where even small private activities were regarded as capitalist danger, as well as in Bulgaria and Albania. For Hungary, Poland, and Yugoslavia the illegal and semi-legal private economy has fulfilled a rather positive role in compensating for the poor performance and consumer services of the official sector. It would be misleading, however, to think that the "legalization" of the shadow private sector is a simple policy task. To acquire "western" attitudes, or a sense of obligation at the individual level, on issues such as tax payments, for example, will not be easy. The absence of such attitudes will surely complicate the attempts of the new governments to revive their private sectors.

PRIVATIZATION STRATEGIES

Although privatization is an unequivocal policy objective throughout the region, a debate has arisen over which of several competing strategies will be most successful. Moreover, there is no obvious answer to the question of exactly what to privatize. Defining property rights, which must be done before property can be privatized, has proven difficult. State property is an uncertain concept, especially if it dominates the whole economy. In fact, property rights are dispersed among state organs, enterprise association managers, and enterprise managers. The situation can be even more confusing in countries where privatization has been preceded by some sort of socialist economic reform, such as in Yugoslavia, Hungary during the reforms of 1968, and Poland during the reforms of 1982.

Privatization should be a dynamic process for which Eastern Europe employs techniques that will allow the rapid transfer of assets from state to private hands. Unlike advanced industrial nations such as Great Britain, Eastern Europe cannot afford to privatize a small percentage of national assets over a decade. Eastern European nations are currently examining the following policy options:

1. *Employee Ownership.* According to this view, distribution of the enterprise's property to its employees would secure a substantial increase in efficiency. The employees are supposed to have an obvious right to the property of the state enterprises that employ them. Not surprisingly, it is mainly propagated by people with some kind of socialist sentiment.

2. *The "Give-Away" Concept.* According to this concept state property belongs to its citizens. Therefore, the first goal of privatization should be the free distribution of the property among the whole population. Employees outside of the sectors being privatized would thus face no discrimination.

3. *The "British Way."* Following the model of Britain's privatization, state property should be privatized by appropriate state organs through open and transparent selling procedures.

4. *Holding Concepts.* Some government officials, realizing that privatization will probably take longer than initially expected, have opted for some intermediary solutions in order to accelerate property reform. Common among them is an effort to identify institutional owners for the transition period. In some cases these would be artificially created state holdings in charge of managing and privatizing the assets. In other cases insurance companies and nonprofit organizations—foundations, universities, and hospitals, for example—would be satisfactory caretakers. Leasing state firms through competitive bidding is another intermediate form of accelerating ownership restructuring.

5. *"Small Privatization."* Although the notion comes from Poland, the idea has been widespread. While other privatization concepts tend to concentrate on the existing, usually large, organizations, this view emphasizes the significance of the organic establishment of new, small private firms. In the extreme version, this way of thinking neglects "big privatization" and tends to believe that the real reserves of efficiency improvement are only in the newly established private firms.

6. *Reprivatization.* Some politicians and scholars advocate reestablishing the property structures that existed prior to the major nationalization campaigns of the 1940s and 1950s. Two major cases are worth mentioning: the Hungarian Smallholders' Party advocated the reprivatization of land in its election campaign in the spring of 1990; and some reprivatization has been permitted in the former German Democratic Republic because of the political circumstances of reunification.

While before the collapse of the communist regimes *reprivatization* was not an issue—and from the point of view of economic rationality it is clearly inferior to many other ways of privatization—it became so after the political upheaval in almost all countries of the region. Reprivatization legislation tries to strike a balance between morally justifiable restitution claims and economic rationality. The East German solution to the issue is that if someone cannot reclaim his or her assets because those assets have changed hands physically so often over the course of the last decades or because they are already privatized, the former owner is entitled to financial compensation.

The Hungarian Restitution Act also favors the principle of compensation, but with limits: a digressive scale and a ceiling of 5 million forints (approximately US$80,000). Moreover, the act offers restitution not in cash but in ownership "vouchers," which can be spent on purchasing assets in privatizing firms. The inflationary impact of creation of these quasi-securities is expected to be less than that of cash compensation. The act treats the peasants preferentially (because of active political lobbying on the part of the Smallholders' Party), a situation later deemed to be unconstitutional by the Constitutional Court. Therefore, the act must be reshaped; either the restitution principle as a whole should be radicalized, with all attendant unfavorable impact on the financial balance of the economy, or land reprivatization should be restricted to the level of restitution of other items.

Restitution laws have been adopted in most of the other post-communist countries as well. The notable exception is Poland, primarily for political reasons, including the fact that the rural reprivatization lobby is weak in Poland because communists did not nationalize most of the land. Still, in the spring of 1991 reprivatization became a political issue far beyond its economic significance.

In contrast to reprivatization, employee ownership was more the focus of ownership reform debates before the political "big bang." The revolution swept away obstacles to an ideologically unlimited privatization debate, rendering half-way employee stock ownership programs unnecessary. The only exception might be parts Yugoslavia, where employee self-management has deep social roots. The self-management movement has shown considerable resistance to alternative privatization methods in Poland, and subsequently did not receive a substantially larger role in Polish reform legislation than elsewhere.

Recent policy debates in most countries of the region have concluded that some unconventional mechanisms must be adopted if privatization is to be a quick and dynamic process. Two major philosophies compete in policy reform: Poland and Czechoslovakia appear to favor mass privatization through some sort of free distribution of state capital shares (without practical results as yet), while in Hungary the practice of spontaneous privatization remains the steadier path.

Paths Pursued by Poland, Hungary, and Czechoslovakia

The privatization strategies being adopted in Poland, Hungary, and Czechoslovakia no doubt reflect each country's domestic political context. Both Hungary and Poland, for example, have previous experience with so-called spontaneous privatization, but the strategy has a better reputation in Hungary.

At the end of the communist era, the process of spontaneous privatization appeared in both Poland and Hungary. In Poland the Solidarity establishment opposed the way enterprise managers and other parts of the former elite acquired state property through the foundation of limited companies. After winning power, the Solidarity-led government stopped this practice and announced a privatization program, thus ending spontaneous privatization.

In Hungary, however, spontaneous privatization has been viewed more favorably. Despite public worry, the process has produced thousands of new corporate structures and brought in more than US$500 million in foreign business investments. It is true that spontaneous privatization has been a corrupt process in many cases, because the decision to transform an enterprise's ownership has belonged to the enterprise managers. Sales may thus have been underpriced, bidding has not been a requisite part of the transaction, and managers have been able to choose their own partners. Another problem with spontaneous transformation is that assets and liabilities have been divided in many cases; state enterprises have taken only valuable assets with them into the new corporate structures, usually leaving the liabilities in empty state holdings. Also, decentralized sales do not allow the state to earn much revenue for its budget.

Spontaneous privatization does, however, have a few benefits. It provided a channel for foreign investment in Hungary. The strengthening of managers' positions that has occurred as a result of such privatization can also be viewed as a virtue. Only the enterprise manager is in the position to anticipate the firm's future direction. In the typical "nobody's ownership" situation of the socialist economy, such knowledge is extremely precious and should be rewarded by preferential access to the assets if rapid efficiency improvement is to be achieved.

Spontaneous privatization has also allowed a cost-free way of decentralizing industrial and trade organizations. The accusation that spontaneous privatization breeds cheap sales and corruption is weak in the sense that any rapid sale of assets as part of widescale privatization would face similar criticism. Civil servants are not immune to corruption; in fact, they are often more vulnerable to it because they know less than their managers about the firms.

Privatization efforts are moving at varying speeds in other Eastern European nations. In Poland the radically pro-capitalist government has failed to accelerate privatization as it had hoped. In the Balkan part of the region major public resistance has dramatically slowed the process. In the spring of 1990 Romanian workers repeatedly expressed their disapproval of sales of factories to Westerners. Expressing collectivist values of this sort is almost unknown in Hungary. Foreign direct investment and corporate transformation of the large state firms will be a much slower process in Romania, Bulgaria, and probably also in the southern and eastern regions of Yugoslavia than in Hungary. The expansion of small private ownership is still likely, as it is a politically far less contentious and far easier process.

In Czechoslovakia the political environment for privatization remains foggy. The country pursued the most orthodox communist economic policy before its velvet revolution at the end of 1989. Nonetheless, the key economic positions in the new federal government went to strongly pro-capitalist politicians. The new political forces have yet to stabilize. The powers of the federal government in the eyes of the republics, especially Slovakia, are not yet certain. Neither is the reaction of the population, educated in a strongly egalitarian manner, to aggressively pro-capitalist policies.

The policy suggested by Minister of Finance Vaclav Klaus advocates a mixture of spontaneous privatization and give-away methods, though the latter strategy is better publicized because of its originality. Under this scheme Czechoslovaks would receive vouchers to be spent on shares of state enterprises. The rest of the assets would be sold by the enterprise's board of directors, as the rights of the property agency would be delegated to these boards, providing the decentralized element of the Czechoslovak privatization scheme. Of course, it will be difficult to find appropriate people to fill the boards, and corruption will not be easily avoided in the privatization process. The government is wary of the potential negative side effects, and it rightly wants to minimize corruption that results from giving preference to board members to acquire shares. Such a policy, however, may be politically sticky. How will the public react if, when trading in shares begins, shares become concentrated in the hands of a few? Due to the lack of appropriate information about the firms, as well as the very low level of the populace's economic education, the losers will be very disappointed.

There is a conviction among some politicians and analysts that political willingness to privatize will be firm and long-lasting, at least in Poland, Hungary, and Czechoslovakia. Indeed, the economic pressure will exist for quite some time. I expect, however, that the vested interests of the new political elite will seriously decrease its determination to implement policies that could risk losing votes. The ambiguity of the Czechoslovak situation has already been mentioned. The political culture in Poland also raises some doubts, and trade union populism might become an organized force against rapid privatization. Also, in Hungary the governing party has a strong populist wing; the governing apparatus, too, has a natural interest in managing the enterprises. After all, this is a power basis of the elite and the apparatus functions just like in other countries with a strong public sector.

OUTLOOK

As mentioned above, spontaneous privatization seems to be a relatively good compromise. On the other hand, lessons learned on the road to privatization necessitate modification of the legal framework.

In Hungary the government has several policy options to correct the weaknesses in the existing legislation that were revealed by spontaneous privatization. Indeed, corrective laws were implemented, such as one creating the State Property Agency in March 1990, as a means to control property transactions. The agency can also initiate and organize "privatization from above," called "active privatization" in the Hungarian professional language.

Political changes after the elections have modified the environment of privatization in Hungary. "Multi-channel privatization" has become the name of the game. Spontaneous privatization has slowed under heavy criticism but has not stopped. Some uncertainties of the legal framework of spontaneous privatization still exist, because the government wants to abolish the enterprise councils that have been the institutional catalysts of the process. Management has manipulated council decisions and thus has strongly influenced the transformations. It is not clear what will replace the enterprise councils.

Small privatization is being prepared, but the resistance of enterprise centers in the affected fields (trade and services) still slows the legislative work. However, draft laws were written by late 1989. Small privatization is crucial for supporting the strengthening of a small, domestic capitalist class. Active privatization (the British model) will be used simultaneously and is particularly important in Hungary, which is burdened by a large domestic state debt (at the beginning of 1991 1300 billion forints, about US$20 billion), one that can be reduced by using funds collected from selling shares to the public.

Crisis management through privatization is also typical in Hungary. Payment arrears of enterprises are now a widespread phenomena in the Hungarian economy, and to date no satisfactory solution has been found. Some skepticism about the widespread use of bankruptcy as a threat is justified, because many state enterprises are not able, nor are they willing, to strengthen their financial discipline. A rigorous bankruptcy procedure would result in massive unemployment and a consequent decline in production. The problem will probably be aggravated by the transformation of trade with the Soviet Union to a dollar basis, as well as by the sharp increase in oil prices. A useful policy tool would be to restructure and sell to financially strong foreign firms the major trouble enterprises (especially ones with strong Soviet export interests), even for below-market prices.

Poland incorporated different channels of privatization into its privatization bill of July 13, 1990. Spontaneous privatization remains, however, very narrow. By law, foreigners may only purchase 10 percent of the shares, though exceptions are likely to be permitted. These two limitations lead me to predict a slow process, though the first cases will happen rather soon. On the other hand, the government is vulnerable to political fights, and advocates of dominant worker ownership still hold a chance of gaining political ground.

Small privatization has begun in Czechoslovakia, while large enterprises are beginning to privatize in 1991. Enterprise councils will probably be the engines of spontaneous privatization, and in the medium run the pro-capitalist wing of the government is also vulnerable.   Liquidity troubles at some big industrial conglomerates are to be expected simultaneously with the onset of ownership reform because of turbulent trade relations with the Soviet Union. These difficulties can decrease the attractiveness of such firms as potential investors.

Crisis phenomena will increase the supply of the Eastern European enterprises to foreign firms.   The relative losers will be those countries in which populist sentiment will excessively hinder underpriced transactions.   Even without major political obstacles, however, the regeneration of a viable property structure will take a long time.   Transactions, as well as entrepreneurial and technical education, are time consuming.

2

Hungary's
Economic Transformation

Catherine M. Sokil

Hungary's recent political transformation from one-party Communist rule to a multiparty democracy has triggered an equally unprecedented economic transformation, from the postwar centrally planned economy toward a market system. Hungary's economic reform experience, which began in 1968 with the New Economic Mechanism, is the longest running in Eastern Europe. However, prior to the events of 1988–1989, these proceeded under severe political constraints, including Communist Party loyalty to the Soviet Union. Despite the removal of these political restraints, economic reform in Hungary remains burdened by the political process of transformation itself.

There is no model for this transformation; indeed, each reforming country in East Central Europe appears to be developing a model specific to its own political, social, and economic circumstances. Certainly, Hungary has not chosen the "shock-therapy" path adopted in Poland. Rather, political discussions in Hungary have produced an alternative approach, which may be called a "consensus program" because it relies on gradual liberalization (Koves and Marer 1990). In the meantime, a comprehensive program for Hungary's transformation has been articulated by a multilateral Blue Ribbon Commission (BRC) with Hungarian participation. It remains to be seen, however, whether the new government in Hungary will implement this program, including its timetable, or whether progress will be further slowed by the political and social costs of the transition, as perceived by an increasingly vocal domestic population. Developments to date, including the new government's announced short-term economic program, suggest that progress toward a market economy will continue cautiously.

WHERE ARE WE NOW?

Hungary suffers from stagnant growth, a staggering government debt (over 55 percent of gross domestic product), a US$20 billion foreign debt burden (US$2,000 per capita), and inflation on the order of 25–30 percent per annum. Recent tax hikes have reduced the incentive for workers and businesses to boost their profits.[1] With a zero population growth as well as a shortage of domestic capital, Hungary joins the ranks of East Central European countries that are actively seeking Western capital, especially equity capital, to help finance the transition. In return, Hungary's leadership promises rewards based on the country's commitment to political and economic democracy.

Hungary's longer reform experience does give it a head start among the other countries of East Central Europe in attracting foreign capital. Chief among the incentives to invest in Hungary compared to its Eastern European neighbors may be its relatively closer trade and business ties with the West; membership in the International Monetary Fund (IMF) and World Bank since 1982; a more developed banking system; and a greater number of managers trained in Western management techniques both at home and abroad. Admittedly, "[w]ith her 27,000 square miles and ten and a half million inhabitants [Hungary] is not the giant market" (Bacskai 1989). But Hungary's location at the geographical, cultural, and political crossroads of Europe; the potential cheap trans-

---

1. Among the taxes: a 53 percent payroll tax (43 percent paid by the employer, 10 percent by the employee); a 50 percent marginal income tax rate; a 40 percent corporate profits tax; a value-added tax (VAT) of up to 25 percent, and other specific excise taxes (BRC, 55).

port provided by the Danube River;[2] and a relatively cheap but skilled labor force appear to be its major competitive advantages.

Legal and other institutions also promote Hungarian enterprises as joint-venture partners. The Hungarian Chamber of Commerce publishes a list of Hungarian companies interested in joint-venture partners, and other similar publications, and sponsors trade exhibits, such as "Discover Hungary: New Business Opportunities" at the World Trade Center in New York in October 1990, which exhort foreigners to the Hungarian market.[3] Indeed, the perceptions by foreign business leaders of the Hungarian leadership's commitment to reform may be responsible for Hungary's recent exemplary success in attracting Western joint-venture partners.[4] Favorable joint-venture and tax laws, such as a 100 percent tax exemption for certain foreign investments deemed of national importance,[5] no doubt also contribute to Hungary's favorable international image.

HOW DID WE GET HERE?

Forty years of imposed centrally planned socialism have left the Hungarian economy weak. The two immediate postwar decades were characterized by unbalanced, extensive economic growth and heavy industrialization achieved through ambitious capital investment along the Stalinist model. For the next two decades, Hungary's New Economic Mechanism only partially revamped the command model. Economic reforms involved changing the instruments of central planning from quantitative directives to finan-

2. Bacskai (1989) makes much of this potential, based on historical as well as future developments. He cites an anticipated network of "off-shore" customs-free zones along the river, the establishment of which would be accelerated by Budapest and Vienna hosting the World Expo in 1998.

3. The former is *Proposals for Joint Ventures* (1989). Other publications include *Invest in Hungary*, published by Interpress Publicity Printing House in Budapest, and *Business Directory 1990*, another Hungarian Chamber of Commerce publication.

4. Nonetheless, the US$800 million in foreign investment in 2,000 joint ventures to date does not meet the government's expectations (Domany 1990).

5. These activities include electronics, automobile/components production, machine-tool production, agriculture and food processing, engineering industries, packaging, pharmaceuticals, energy- and waste-saving products, telecommunications, tourism, and biotechnology.

cial "regulators," including prices, wage rules, exchange rates, interest rates, and taxes. Although well intentioned, the changes represented only minimal progress toward a "market," for they had only a limited impact on the decentralization of economic decisionmaking power. The legacies of the centrally planned system remained, including constraints of political and economic commitments to the Soviet Union, Communist Party domination of the economy, and extreme concentration of economic power in huge monopoly firms. Despite the professed goal of some form of "market socialism," these constraints were severe enough to preclude the development of any real "market system," a goal now made possible by the political transformation.

The turning point for Hungary very likely was July 1989, when the Hungarian Socialist Workers' Party, the Opposition political parties, and the Third Side (comprised of a variety of social and political groups), began to discuss the peaceful transition of the political and economic system to a multiparty democracy and market economy. However, what precisely is meant by a "market system," and just how "capitalist" Hungary is likely to become depends on the resolution of a number of questions of social and economic policy. A short historical digression will help clarify Hungary's progress toward deconcentrated competition—a "market"—until now, obstacles encountered to date, and potential problems.

In 1982 various new forms of second-economy activities either were introduced or revived, creating a continuum of various "mixed" forms of enterprises in Hungary. The forms could be distinguished on the basis of the degree of regulation by authorities. The first economy was composed of the heavily regulated state and large traditional cooperative sectors. The freer second economy, or the nonsocialist sector, was comprised of new entrepreneurial forms, including small cooperatives, the private sector (legal and illegal), and the so-called combined forms of enterprise (for example, joint ventures and leasing).

The introduction of these new entrepreneurial forms created the "half-way house" of Hungarian reform, characterized by remarkable growth of the second economy but various perverse economic behaviors and limited competition.[6] The majority of Hungarian

6. See Sokil (1990) for details.

citizens participated in the second economy, often in addition to their first-economy jobs. In terms of numbers of people involved, the enterprise contract work association (ECWA)—groups of employees hired by the state enterprise to work after hours at unrestricted wages—became by far the most widespread of the new forms. By hiring workers under the ECWA system, the state enterprise could keep its best workers and prevent them from being bid away by other state enterprises. This system, ironically, acted to accentuate the perverse incentives of the planned economy: workers were more likely to shirk regular-time work and to put more effort into overtime.

The new enterprise forms resulted in unequal competition between the first and second economy. The first economy had all the trappings of the typical centrally planned economy (CPE): management of enterprises appointed by ministries, and therefore accountable to them, but with the well-known "soft budget constraint."[7] The second-economy forms enjoyed managerial independence but were subjected to a "hard budget constraint." Given the different stringencies of their constraints, these new forms were more responsive to markets and prices. The second economy had more restricted access to capital and material inputs but an advantageous access to labor. Many workers kept their first-economy job for the perquisites that state enterprises had to provide their employees, but they worked much harder at their private-sector jobs. In other words, the mere existence of these parallel economy forms did not guarantee progress in the development of true competition, which is an important prerequisite of a functioning "market mechanism."

Regulations were uncertain and ever-changing in both sectors, with the paradoxical result that socialist firms became even less profit oriented, and nonsocialist firms more, at least in the short run. Due to the absence of a capital market that would allow reinvestment of profits in the second economy, size restrictions on the

7. The "soft budget constraint," a term attributed to Hungarian economist János Kornai, refers to the fact that under a centrally planned system many of the financial constraints (taxes and wage rules, for example) imposed on the firm by central authorities are not binding. In the event of failure to comply, or even financial insolvency, authorities have no choice but to accept noncompliance and, in the extreme case, to "bail out" the firm.

second economy, and the uncertainty of regulation, second-economy enterprises tended to use profits to increase wages and bonuses. The "conspicuous consumption" of these private incomes elicited the envy of workers who either voluntarily or involuntarily were confined to the socialist sector. The mentality of "Grab the profits while you can" (Marer 1989) contributed to popular negative perceptions of the "market" and of entrepreneurship—perceptions that the new political leadership in Hungary, now accountable to the population at large, must consider very seriously.

In response to these problems, the period up to 1989 saw the establishment in Hungary of some of the necessary preconditions for freer competition between the state and private sectors. These involved reforms within the socialist sector to reduce the central controls on it; reforms to promote and expand the second-economy forms; and reforms to equalize competition between the socialist and nonsocialist sectors. The latter included capital market reforms involving the development of institutions and instruments that would service both, and labor market reforms that would reduce wage controls in the state sector. Among the developments to promote competition were the following milestones:

> 1979: Rules for establishing subsidiaries and new production ventures were eased, and a deconcentration program instituted to break up some monopolies. (Still, Hungarian industry remains one of the world's most concentrated.)

> 1980: A so-called competitive pricing system was established to link domestic and world market prices. In practice, prices were determined through negotiation between the enterprise and the National Materials and Prices Office (NMPO), the body responsible for price formation.

> Three industrial sector ministries were consolidated into one Ministry of Industry, with less direct intervention authority.

> 1982–1983: Production profile restrictions[8] of enterprises were relaxed, to promote entry. (In 1985, these were eliminated completely.)

8. "Profile restrictions" refer to the quality and assortment of products that under the traditional centrally planned system are typically prescribed. Or, at least there is little or no incentive to vary assortment, improve quality, or innovate.

1983: Enterprises began filling important managerial positions through advertised public tenders.

1983: Enterprises were given the right to issue bonds to raise capital.

1985: The managerial system of state enterprises was reformed. Legal authority relating to production inputs, marketing, investment, and human resource management (i.e., most managerial functions) was formally delegated to enterprise management, which as of 1985 came under one of the following three schemes:

1. For public utilities and strategically important firms, the traditional management system (directly responsible to the ministry) remained;

2. For firms with fewer than 500 employees, the general assembly of workers became the management authority; and

3. For all other firms with over 500 employees (80% of state enterprises), an elected enterprise council consisting of representatives of workers (50%) and management (50%) became the new managerial authority. These representatives would elect and supervise the enterprise director, subject to the approval of the authorities. Despite the management system changes, formal ownership of the assets of the enterprise remained in state hands.

1986: A Bankruptcy Law was enacted.

1986: Foreign trade rights were extended to many enterprises.

1987: A two-tier banking system was established. Specialized new financial institutions serviced industrial, agricultural, and consumer cooperatives, but these faced practical limits to the capital they could raise, relative to the commercial banks which were refinanced by the central bank.

1988: A tax reform was implemented, instituting a value-added tax (VAT) and a personal income tax (PIT). (Marer 1989)

Still, unequal competition of the second economy for resources could be attributed not only to labor and capital market imperfections, but also to unequal taxation[9] and legal status. In 1989 three important laws were introduced to promote entry and to put all enterprises on equal legal footing.

1. Act VI of 1988, The Law on Economic Associations, or The Company Act *(In Effect as of January 1, 1989)*

This law allows freedom of enterprise: anyone, including private persons, may form a business association simply by registering it. Contrary to past practice, no approval of the Ministry of Finance or local councils is required. The Law on Economic Associations represents the first legal code that uniformly governs and regulates all forms of "business companies" or economic associations and thus strives to create equal competition among all enterprise forms.

Patterned after the West German model, the act recognizes six company forms that may be formed on an equal legal and tax footing by both domestic and foreign legal entities and/or individuals. These are listed in Table 2-1, from simplest to most complicated. The act is a watershed in that it formally allows private and mixed capital ownership and eases foreign direct investment, though the details of the latter are left to a subsequent act. The act expressly does not extend to state enterprises, state farms, and cooperatives (small and large, including agricultural)—these would operate parallel to the six forms, pending the subsequent Transformation Act.

2. Act XXIV of 1988, On Foreign Investment in Hungary *(In Effect as of January 1, 1989)*

This act allows companies to be 100 percent foreign-owned, and allows special tax exemptions to be granted to them (including a 100 percent tax exemption for foreign investment in the fields listed

---

9. For example, the tax reform that introduced a personal income tax on January 1, 1988, was detrimental to the private sector because of the high marginal rates of taxation. Indeed, the PIT was introduced in response to high second-economy incomes, and it was strongly biased against overtime work, as wages above the average were taxed at high marginal rates. Many private enterprises shut down as a result.

Table 2-1. Company Forms in Hungary as of 1989

---

1. Unlimited Partnership
2. Deposit (Limited) Partnership
3. Union
4. Joint Enterprise
5. Limited Liability Company (LLC)
6. Company Limited by Shares (Co., Ltd.)

Note: In the "company limited by shares," only current and past employees of the company could own shares. One-person companies limited by shares could be established, provided the founder is the state or a banking institution. The Act also contains provisions for advance public notice of a "takeover" of one company by another, to preclude Western-style "surprise [hostile?] takeovers." Foreigners are free to buy shares in any company, provided its shares are registered and the foreigner does not acquire a controlling interest in a limited liability company without a special permit.

previously). The law also protects the foreign investor from nationalization or expropriation of an investment.

3. Act XIII of 1989, On the Transformation of Economic Organizations and Economic Associations, or The Transformation Act
(In Effect as of May 30, 1990)

The Transformation Act supplements the Act on Economic Associations. Transformation is defined as a situation in which "an economic entity changes completely, without liquidation, into an economic association." The Transformation Act envisions the transformation of *existing* state enterprises and cooperatives into economic associations (companies). An important element to transformation is a valuation of the enterprise to be presented in a *balance of property and liabilities* and to be confirmed by independent audit. The act admits to not being an ownership reform, suggesting that this will be the next step in the evolution of legal provisions governing the regulation, management, and ownership of enterprises in Hungary.

In addition to these three laws, 1989 saw the implementation of a New Accounting System Law requiring all firms of a certain size to employ Western accounting and bookkeeping practices (Wolfe and Poor 1990), and an Unemployment Law, establishing rules for unemployment benefits.

The Hungarian and Western press had a field day reporting some of the implications of the new laws. By June 1989 170 companies had transformed themselves into joint-stock companies (Hunyadi 1990). Novotrade, Hungary's first joint-stock company, in 1989 encouraged its top management to buy shares and take shares in lieu of bonuses. Shares of transformed joint-stock companies today trade on the Budapest stock market.

Meanwhile, 1989 also saw the development of many institutions of a politically and economically democratic society. The Law on Strikes—viewed as important to creating countervailing power to the power of management in a market economy—was passed, permitting workers to strike in the event of failure of employees and management to negotiate a settlement. The Parliament formally legalized opposition political parties, and opposition groups were allowed to operate as associations legally under the new Law on Economic Associations. The Law on Political Parties banned parties from organizing at the workplace and ordered the ruling Socialist Party to start disbanding its cells in the workplace— heretofore a key element of party control over workers and management in CPEs known as the *nomenklatura* system.

WHERE ARE WE? A RECAP

It appears that Hungary has progressed along three avenues of decentralization of productive economic power simultaneously.

1. One avenue, widely and rather successfully used in Hungary to date, has been to allow new enterprises to multiply, based on private gain and free of the political legacies of the centrally planned system. Progress in the development of labor and capital markets has helped to equalize competition for factors of

production. The Law on Economic Associations essentially allows any Hungarian citizen to start a company and formally puts all enterprises on equal legal footing, and the Law on Transformation allows state enterprises to transform themselves into joint-stock companies that might be (at least partly) privately owned (by foreign or domestic citizens). Political democracy is an important element in the continuing process of convincing the populace that the change in attitude toward entrepreneurial undertakings is real and lasting, thus reducing the incentives for "conspicuous consumption."

2. A second avenue is to liberalize the first economy, or the state/socialist sector itself, from the constraints of the past. Progress has been made, aided by the 1989 laws on Economic Association and Transformation. Very significantly, political parties—notably the Hungarian Socialist Party (HSP, formerly the Hungarian Communist Party)—have been banned from organizing at the workplace.

3. A third, complementary avenue is to attract competition from abroad through joint ventures and direct foreign investment. As of 1989 Hungary allows 100 percent foreign ownership of firms and repatriation of convertible currency profit up to the value of the investment. Hungary has attracted many joint ventures; even the American Ambassador to Hungary, Mark Palmer, resigned his post to get in on the joint-venture action. The most publicized foreign purchase of a Hungarian firm to date has been General Electric's purchase of a majority share of Tungsram, a manufacturer of light bulbs, lamps, and robot controls. George Soros, a Hungarian émigré, established a New York–based venture capital fund to invest in Hungary. Despite uncertain returns, investors felt assured of limited downside risk and the issue was oversubscribed.

Although legal provisions have created a more flexible framework for private initiative in Hungary, the ownership structure of most enterprises is still vague. The reforms to date do not designate an individual or institution to have full property rights—that is, the right to manage the assets and appropriate the returns on them—if not ministry-appointed representatives of the state.

After twenty years of attempting to reform socialism, the

Hungarian leadership is now committed to a full-scale restructuring of the ownership system, though the details and pace are uncertain. What is certain is that the process has been slowed by the problems associated with privatizations to date in Hungary. Indeed, though all of the major parties in Hungary favor some form of privatization, they have protested against the method by which privatization has occurred up to now. They have accused existing managers and HSP members of private profiteering from the sales of state-owned companies at depressed prices in spontaneous privatizations.[10] What caused these problems?

Recall that in 1985 management system changes involved placing about 80 percent of state enterprises under the managerial authority of the enterprise council, composed 50 percent of elected representatives of workers and 50 percent of elected representatives of management. The managerial changes involving greater devolution of managerial authority to workers was seen as a temporary solution only, offered in the interest of wresting authority out of the hands of government bureaucrats. Given introduction of the legal institutions making private ownership possible, the enterprise councils became very powerful.

The Act on Economic Associations and the Act on Transformation provided the legal foundations for the limited privatization of state enterprises. However, abuses of the legal possibilities arose in several cases, because the decision to privatize and the valuation of the enterprise to be sold off were determined by the enterprise councils. In the absence of a true capital market to value assets, powerful figures with access to undervalued shares could abuse the system. In short, enterprise councils were capable of enriching themselves and their friends by allowing state assets to be sold at bargain prices. Privatizations were subsequently limited pending renationalization, as ownership rights that had been given to workers' councils are essentially given back to the state, a development that can appear to be a temporary step backwards.

The issue of privatization has raised many unanswered questions. Should unprofitable companies be restructured before or after privatization? How can the Hungarian leadership realistically get domestic citizens to be part of the privatization process, despite a

10. See, for example, *Hungary Today*, October 1989.

shortage of domestic capital? Should domestic or foreign citizens receive preferential treatment, or neither? How will monopoly and oligopoly industries be affected by privatization? Who should receive the proceeds of privatization, and how should these be used?

As of the March 1990 elections all of the major political parties favored some type of privatization, acknowledging that the half-way house of economic reform under predominantly state ownership had been unsuccessful. The platform of the Alliance of Free Democrats was the most ambitious, calling for three-quarters of Hungary's 2,700 state enterprises to be privatized over three to five years. Alternative paths to resolution of the thorny ownership issue were suggested. One suggestion was predominantly state ownership of the now transformed companies, via some organ to operate the state's shares. Another suggestion was to establish state holding companies that would be owned and controlled by various social organizations, such as municipalities, nonprofit organizations (schools, hospitals), the social security fund and other pension systems, insurance companies, universities, and foundations. In other words, state ownership would be replaced by ownership by collective social organizations that would compete on the stock market. Finally, reprivatization could occur through direct sale or distribution of shares of enterprises to workers or to the public. In the absence of sufficient domestic capital to purchase shares, many people have suggested distributing shares to the population and/or workers for free or for only a fraction of the money down.

WHERE ARE WE HEADED?

The outcome of Hungary's elections will bear heavily on the evolving issue of ownership. The March 1990 Parliamentary elections resulted in a coalition government led by Prime Minister Jozsef Antall of the center-right Hungarian Democratic Forum (which holds 164 of 386 seats), with the "Western-style liberal" (Domany 1990) Alliance of Free Democrats constituting the major opposition party (92 of 386 seats).

In anticipation of the parliamentary elections, the Blue Ribbon Commission was organized to advise the new government and to provide it with an integrated program for the transformation to a

market economy—in short, to provide input into the economic plat-
form of whatever party prevailed in the parliamentary elections.
The chief Western organizers of the effort included the Hudson
Institute, an Indianapolis-based think tank, and the East-West
Forum, the Bronfman Foundation's policy center (Chapman 1990).

The BRC report recommended a comprehensive, "preannounced
path and a firm timetable" for the transition. To quote the report:

> Once a government has defined its objectives clearly, it must
> implement change in quantum leaps. . . . Slowness can cause
> the early consensus supporting the government's program to
> collapse before implementation is completed. . . . A govern-
> ment need not have broad public support for each specific re-
> form measure [which] leads to excessive compromise that
> emasculates a comprehensive program. (BRC 1990)

The BRC conceded that the appropriate stage for caution is the policy deliberation phase, during which alternative proposals are considered; it was hoped, therefore, that the work of the BRC would
save the new government much-needed time during precisely this
stage, especially by providing a separate set of recommendations on
the government's first one hundred days in office.

On the issue of privatization, the BRC report recommended that:

> Practically all retail trade, service establishments, workshops and
> similar sized firms should be privatized within one year. . . .
> Parent companies should be forced to sell their outlets and
> shops to private buyers who will obtain real assets in exchange
> for real payment obligations. . . . A new Act on Agricultural
> Land . . . [should] guarantee the right of private ownership and
> the right to dispose of land.

The report estimated the book value of all state-owned enterprises
in Hungary to be about 2,000 billion forints (approximately US$30
billion), and the current annual flow of private currency savings
available for purchasing assets (other than real estate) to be not
more than 20 billion forints (US$300 million) per year. At this
rate of domestic savings, the report continues, "it would take
Hungarians a hundred years to purchase all state enterprises." In
addition to promoting means to attract foreign capital, the BRC
suggests expanding the domestic ownership base by special lines of

credit to Hungarian citizens and by recommending sales and/or placements to pension funds, mutual funds, nonprofit foundations, local governments, insurance companies, and the like (BRC, 27).

The BRC recommends a three-step process for privatization: (1) an independent private company (Hungarian or foreign) should evaluate and prepare a prospectus disclosing full information about the company to be privatized, (2) another independent company (an investment bank) should seek prospective buyers and negotiate the sale, and (3) a government agency should monitor the process and report to Parliament on it.

The BRC also recommends modifications in the State Property Agency (SPA), founded on March 1, 1990, under the January Law on Protection of Property Entrusted to State Enterprises. This agency, designed to monitor the privatization process and correct the abuses of spontaneous privatizations, was placed directly under Parliament's jurisdiction. The BRC recommends that Parliament set broad guidelines for and monitor the implementation of the privatization program but that the details be delegated to a new privatization agency that is "self-standing within the government" (BRC, 28).

According to at least one member of the Hungarian Parliament, the BRC proposal is likely to be implemented, because "there is no other proposal."[11] Indeed, leaders of the two major political parties—the Hungarian Democratic Forum and the Alliance of Free Democrats—were members of the BRC and signed the report (Chapman 1990). However, the timetable is likely to be delayed due to the politics of the transformation—including the relatively prominent position of members of the Free Democratic Party on the BRC.[12]

For now, Hungary's new government appears to have put economics on the back burner as it adjusts itself to the new political climate of post-1989 East Central Europe. The government's short-term economic program announced on June 29, 1990, effective July 1, has been criticized as only scratching the surface without providing fundamental cures for the country's domestic economic ills.

11. Based on my own conversations with a member of Parliament during the summer of 1990.
12. For example, Dr. Marton Tardos, a respected economist and co-chair of the BRC, is a Free Democrat.

The economic goals of the government for now are modest: to reduce the government budget deficit (under the IMF program, it
should be reduced from 27 billion to 10 billion forints) and to reverse the economic downturn in time for a three-year economic
program starting January 1, 1991.[13]

Nonetheless, pronouncements by the central bank state that

> The priority objective of the new Hungarian Government, in of-
> fice since May 23, 1990, is to establish a strong social market
> economy based on private ownership and private enterprise, to
> arrest the growth of external indebtedness and meet all debt
> service obligations on time and accurately, and to maintain the
> creditworthiness of the country." (Vincze and Vitez, various
> years)

Toward that aim, the government set up its Privatization Committee, headed by State Secretary Gyorgy Matolcsy, economic policy
adviser to the prime minister, at the end of July 1990. A privatization program is to start soon and is to be carried out by the
State Property Agency. The goal of the State Property Agency's
First Privatization Program is to sell to the private sector, in
Hungary and abroad, the majority of shares of a selected group of
manufacturing, tourist, commercial, trade, and transport sector enterprises. These enterprises represent US$507 million in total
equity, US$1.1 billion in total assets, US$1.4 billion in annual
sales, and US$92 million in before-tax profits, and they are ex-
pected to generate US$385–615 million in revenues for the state
(FPP 1990). But progress will be slow so long as privatization appears to be tainted with scandal and Hungarian citizens remain
skeptical of the process.[14]

---

13. See *Hungary Today*, July 1990.
14. Each deal's abuses—including sales to former managers and foreign buyers at
bargain prices—have been heavily publicized in the press. For example, when
Vilaggazdasag, an economic daily, published a list of thirty-eight firms, worth about
40 billion forints (over US$600 million), as the first to be privatized, the State
Property Agency and other government officials denied the existence of a list and
accused the daily of false journalism *(MTI Econews*, July 7 and 13, 1990).

REFERENCES

Bacskai, Tamas. 1989. "Why Hungary?" *The Hungarian Economy: A Quarterly Economic and Business Review* 17, 2-4.

Bauer, Tamas. 1988. "Economic Reforms Within vs. Beyond the State Sector." *American Economic Review* 78, 2 (May).

BRC (Blue Ribbon Commission). 1990. *Hungary: In Transformation to Freedom and Prosperity.* Economic Program Proposals of the Joint Hungarian-International Blue Ribbon Commission. Indianapolis, Ind., and Budapest, Hungary, Hudson Institute, April.

Chapman, Bruce. 1990. "A Recipe for a Free-Market Hungary." *Wall Street Journal,* April 6.

Domany, Andras. 1990. "Hungary: A Year of Achievement." *Institutional Investor* 24, 13 (October): 267–70.

FPP (First Privatization Program). 1990. Allami Vagyonügynökség (State Property Agency). Budapest, September.

Hungarian Ministry of Finance. *Public Finance in Hungary,* selected issues, including vol. 54: "Act XIII 1989: On the Transformation of Economic Organizations and Economic Associations (Transformation Act)."

Hungaropress (Economic Information). Hungarian Chamber of Commerce, various issues.

Hunyadi, Csilla, ed. 1990. *Hungary Today* (January).

Koves, Andras, and Paul Marer. 1990. "Economic Liberalization in Eastern Europe and in Market Economies." Draft dated July 1990, to be published in a forthcoming book edited by the authors.

Marer, Paul. 1990. "Lessons of Successful Market Economies and the Political Economy of System Change in Central, Eastern, and Southern Europe." Essay prepared for the Aspen Institute's Congressional Conference on Eastern Europe, Prague, Czechoslovakia, August 26–31.

———. 1989. "Hungary's Political and Economic Transformation (1988–1989) and Prospects after Kadar." U.S. Congress, Joint Economic Committee, *Pressures for Reform in the East European Economies.* Washington, D.C.: Government Printing Office.

Sokil, Catherine M. 1990. "Hungarian Financial and Labor Market Reforms: Developing Conditions for the Market Mechanism?" *Money, Incentives, and Efficiency in the Hungarian Economic*

Reform. Ed. Josef C. Brada and Istvan Dobozi. Armonk, N.Y.: M.E. Sharpe, Inc.

Tardos, Marton. 1989a. "How to Create Markets in Eastern Europe: The Hungarian Case," and Paul Marer comment, chaps. 9 and 11. *Economic Adjustment and Reform in Eastern Europe and the Soviet Union.* Ed. Josef C. Brada, Ed A. Hewett, and T. Wolf. Durham, N.C.: Duke University Press.

———. 1989b. "The Property Rights in Hungary." Undated manuscript.

Vincze, E., and A. Vitez, eds. Various issues. *Economic Bulletin, Market Letter, and Quarterly Review.* National Bank of Hungary.

Wolfe, Joseph, and Jozsef Poor. 1990. "A Socioeconomic Note on Hungary in 1990." Draft V of a Working Paper dated March 6.

3

Poland's Political, Economic, and Social Landscape

Gregory Jedrzejczak

In September 1989 the Solidarity-supported government of Prime Minister Tadeusz Mazowiecki entered office, ending forty-five years of uninterrupted rule by a Communist regime. In a structural dimension, this change resulted in Western-style political and economic institutions. Poland is now directed toward the creation of a multiparty parliamentary democracy and an economy with a large private sector. In Poland these efforts are deeply rooted in long-lasting anticommunist political opposition and in the ethos of the Solidarity movement.

In a practical dimension, on January 1, 1990, the new government introduced a program of radical economic reforms (known as the stabilization program) aimed at ending hyperinflation and creating the legal, institutional, and economic basis for a market economy. Although the program has not been in effect long enough for definitive judgments, a number of external and internal factors have emerged. Externally, the Polish economy has suffered as a result of oil price increases due to the Iraq crisis, the rapid deterioration of the Soviet economy, and the transformation of the former CMEA (Comecon) trading system, including the reunification of Germany. Internal problems include the redefinition of the Polish political system—presidential and parliamentary elections, the waning of Solidarity as a political power, and emerging political parties—and a new wave of social unrest as a result of the end of the political honeymoon enjoyed by the noncommunist government. All in all, the Polish economy is still unstable, but that instability is now due to political events. An examination of economic factors, however, indicates that the Polish economy is slowly but visibly moving toward a market economy.

Section I summarizes the most important political, economic, and social conditions, which constitute the starting point for the transition to a politically democratic society with a market economy. Section II focuses on the assumptions and the early results of the stabilization program. Finally, Section III examines the likely development over the next few years of privatization and capital markets in Poland. I focus at length on the economic factors and their implications for the transition process, treating the sociopolitical dimension as "an active environment."

SECTION I. THE HERITAGE

Political developments in Poland during 1989 amazed the world. The ruling Communist Party was compelled to relinquish its hold on power, partially free elections were held, and the prospect of a Poland governed by fully democratically elected bodies became an achievable goal. At the same time, Poland's experience illustrates the difficulties of transforming a closed, centrally planned and directed society with a distorted economy and inefficient enterprises into an open, democratic society with an efficient, free-market economy. The roots of these difficulties can be found in the early 1950s and even the 1940s, but I will concentrate on the basic tendencies in the 1980s.

Economic Growth

After an economic collapse over the years 1979 to 1982, the Polish economy began in 1983 to recover its potential for economic growth. However, the impact of the first few years of the so-called martial-law economy, which included the automatic reconstruction of the economic system and severe social discipline, caused growth to abate by the late 1980s; indeed, in 1989 the growth rate actually declined to -2 percent.

Inflation

Two features of the inflation process were very characteristic in the 1980s:

1. For the first time in post–World War II history, Polish authorities had to admit that a centrally planned economy (CPE) was definitely vulnerable to uncontrollable price fluctuations. In other words, inflation was "opened" after years of being "hidden."
2. This "opening" was caused by the administration's decision to raise prices in 1982 and 1988 (moves rationalized by an attempt to achieve equilibrium of the consumer market—in other words, socially acceptable shortages of consumer goods), attempts that in both cases were unsuccessful. As a result, Poles have grown used to inflation as a constant phenomenon, and at the same time have grown skeptical of the government's ability to fight it.

Balance of Payments and External Debt

Poland's hard currency, foreign debt burden is the most visible heritage of the centrally planned economy. Poland has the highest convertible currency debt in Eastern Europe, totaling about US$40 billion at the end of 1989, equal to 470 percent of the total exports of goods and services. The debt has grown quickly, almost doubling from about US$26 billion at the end of 1981. This disastrous increase had many causes, including the current-account deficit, the structure of debt maturity, and the depreciation of the U.S. dollar.

More than two-thirds of Poland's convertible currency debt is owed to official bilateral creditors. Since 1981 Poland has run into substantial interest arrears with members of the "Paris Club" of Western creditor nations. Poland kept current on its interest obligations to commercial banks until September 1989, when the new government ceased most interest payments on medium- and long-term obligations to those banks.

Ownership Structure

The distorted ownership structure of the economy is the most intractable remnant of a centrally planned economy, and, consequently, the change of this structure is seen as the most important factor of a successful transformation to a Western-type society.

It is important to remember that the division between the private and public sectors is not clearly defined in the CPE's economic and statistical terminology. To this day, the colorful ideological and confusing terms "socialized" and "unsocialized" economy" are being used. By those definitions, the public sector can mean economic units placed at different stages of state control as well as differentiated legal forms.

The state-owned enterprise is the dominating organizational form of the national economy. Separate laws regulate the legal and financial statutes of the state enterprise, guaranteeing far-reaching organizational and financial independence. The state's interests, within the territory of the state enterprise, are represented by the manager as well as through employee self-management. The interests of the state, as the owner of the enterprise, are represented by the so-called founding organ. In other words, specific ministries represent the state treasury in relation to the largest enterprises, and local governing bodies in relation to the rest of the enterprises. An enterprise easily can have at its disposal all of its assets and can sell them to private parties and invest them in other companies. Without the approval of the founding organ, however, it cannot liquidate itself or restructure itself into a joint-stock company.

One must also include under the umbrella of public ownership the existing service and production cooperatives. The activities of these cooperatives were under strict state control, and the effects of their activities were defined in the state's economic plans.

Forms of government ownership on a small scale can be seen in private and public limited companies, in which state ownership plays a dominant role. A portion of the state's assets are at the disposal of budgetary units and nonprofit organizations.

Symmetrically, the private sector's domain is not clearly marked. Outside of a visible center—in which firms with sole ownership, as well as small, private, limited companies, are placed—we have a gray sphere, which, from the viewpoint of ownership, is diversified. A long period of political and fiscal discrimination against private ownership is the primary reason for this situation. Moreover, in the last few years new rules have allowed a mixture of state and private (both Polish and foreign) capital in the form of companies, as well as through long-term leasing of state assets to private companies. Such a mix has led to the creation of so-called *nomenklatura* limited companies and has resulted in a very serious and still unresolved political problem. However, apart from the expressed reservations, the public sector clearly has a dominating position in the Polish economy. Table 3-1 shows aggregated figures characterizing this phenomenon.

As is evident from the given data, Polish industry is almost completely in the hands of the public sector. Characteristic is relatively small employment in relation to the share of GNP and to the stock of fixed capital. This evolves from the structure of the economy—private industry is concentrated in labor-consuming, quasi-handicraft branches. As a result, the industry's private sector is characterized by a greater number of firms, which are, at the same time, much smaller in terms of the number of employees and engaged capital. On the other hand, the public sector of industry is much more concentrated, which is a typical result of a long-lasting, centrally planned economy.

Agriculture plays an exceptional role in the Polish ownership structure, but as in the case of industry, organizational structure, level of employment, and the overall assets structure (measured by the size of the farm) are differentiated essentially through state and cooperative ownership on one hand, and private ownership on the other.

The building industry represents the second largest domain in the private economy within the national economy. As in the case of industry, there is a clear difference in the organizational spread of activities.

The traditional area of activity in the private sector is providing services for households. In 1989 legal forms of providing private services were developed in education and banking. The possibilities have not yet been taken advantage of significantly.

SECTION II. THE STABILIZATION PROGRAM

The above-mentioned stabilization program was announced in October 1989 and introduced at the beginning of 1990. The philosophy of the program came from the recognition that the Polish economy required fundamental systemic change, and that it would have to be achieved quickly, through radical actions, in order to shorten a transitional stage that is extremely hard on society.

The choice of this approach was also dictated by the fact that the program was launched under extremely adverse social and economic conditions. The economy was in a structural and functional disequilibrium due to a host of factors: the ecological disaster; the housing crisis; the foreign debt burden; the rapid price climb linked with wage explosion; the zloty depreciation; the growing deficit of the state budget; and a decrease in output.

The stabilization program, by its nature, cannot cope with all of the above-mentioned disequilibria. The program introduced measures to bring inflation and the balance of payments under control. Among the most important measures were:

1. rapid devaluation of the zloty close to the level of the uncontrolled parallel market rate;
2. relaxation of restrictions on trade and payments;
3. implementation of monetary and fiscal programs reducing deficit financing of government spending and limiting monetary and credit expansion;
4. substantial increases in taxes, especially in tax-limiting wage increases; and
5. monthly adjustable and positive real interest rates for zloty balances.

The economic situation after six months of stabilization-program implementation is unclear, as the following factors attest:

1. Inflation, after reaching a monthly rate of 78 percent in January, slowed sharply to about 5 percent in March and was stabilized in the next few months.

Table 3-1. Participation of Public and Private Ownership
in the National Economy
(Percentage Share at the End of 1988)

Branches of National Economy		*Forms of Ownership* General	Public[a]	Private
General Economy				
	A	100	81.9	18.1
	B	100	65.5	34.5
	C	100	70.6	29.4
Industry				
	A	100	93.6	6.4
	B	100	88.3	11.7
	C	100	97.9	2.1
Agriculture				
	A	100	29.4	70.6
	B	100	21.1	78.9
	C	100	34.3	65.7
Building				
	A	100	79.2	20.8
	B	100	79.3	20.7
	C	100	90.2	9.8
Transport				
	A	100	NA	NA
	B	100	95.9	4.1
	C	100	99.1	0.9
Commerce				
	A	100	NA	NA
	B	100	93.9	6.1
	C	100	96.8	5.2

a. State-owned + cooperatives.
A = GNP in 1988.
B = Average employment in 1988.
C = Net value of fixed assets (current prices) at the end of 1988.

2. The zloty has remained stable against the dollar after drastic
   devaluation, apparently without intervention by the central
   bank.
3. Interest rates fell from 36 percent per month in January to a
   single-digit number in April and subsequent months.
4. Industrial output fell dramatically in the first two months of
   1990, further declining to about 30 percent below the previous
   year's output.
5. Unemployment, though still at a relatively low level, has increased rapidly from the permanent shortage of labor force to
   about 8 percent of employment in the nonbudgetary sector of
   economy.
6. The state budget deficit improved to a significant surplus two
   months after implementation of the program.
7. External reserves improved from a deficit to a significant surplus of US$2 billion at the end of June 1990.

The key question, however, is to what extent these results,
achieved by macroeconomic measures, will impact positively on the
behavior of such microeconomic players as enterprises, households,
banks, and foreign investors. The answer is not obvious. On the
one hand, to call implemented measures and their results a shock
is an understatement. The basic necessities in Poland had for a
long time come cheap. The price subsidy system and the guaranteed provision of a job meant an adequate existence, an unfearful
and undemanding life. As a result, this transition could be traumatic and even paralyzing for the political and economic activity of
the society. On the other hand, entrepreneurial behavior has begun to manifest itself in rapidly expanding parallel markets, services, and foreign trade.

SECTION III. BEYOND THE STABILIZATION PROGRAM

Economic stabilization is only a prerequisite for success in pursuing
systemic changes aimed at leading economic and social systems
toward a market economy. Two long-term elements will play a
critical role in these changes: (1) privatization, and (2) develop-

ment of capital markets, each of which is examined in detail below.

Privatization

The government's economic program, in its stabilizing context, directed toward fighting inflation, treats privatization as a stimulus for growth in the overall economy. The changes in the structure of ownership in the Polish economy are aimed at transforming the existing structure into a system functioning in highly developed European countries. The comparison of this effort with the data of Table 3-1 shows the scale of the assumed changes in the ownership structure. For example, it is presumed that privatizing 10 percent of the Polish economy equals, in terms of employment, the total number of privatizations in the world carried out up to this day.

An unprecedented scale of privatization shows that this effort, in its intellectual and organizational dimension, is both a macroeconomic and a social problem. The privatization program will open two main roads to ownership changes, the first of which is small privatization. Small privatization includes the creation of workshops, as well as support for growth of the private sector from the bottom. It will be achieved through the creation of new private firms and through the growth of already existing firms. One must, however, note the short-term contradiction between the stabilization program—which calls for limiting the population's real savings and imposing a positive real interest rate—and the capital mobilization needed for privatization.

The second road is portfolio investments, the general framework of which has the following characteristics:

1. a general availability to the public of shares that can be purchased from privatized enterprises;
2. transparency of the privatization procedures, above all the procedure involving the sale of shares;
3. the preference for small, passive investors to spread ownership as broadly as possible; and
4. full transferability of shares on a secondary market.

The Polish citizen is seen as the primary potential buyer of shares, regardless of the place of employment or the legal source of income. The social and political assumption of "citizen share ownership" results in serious economic consequences, specifically an overly broad dispersion of shares in comparison to Western economies.

The employees of privatized enterprises will be a preferred group of buyers who will benefit from a substantial decrease in the sale price of up to 20 percent of all shares issued. However, these preferences will be awarded to individuals and not to the employees as a group.

Attracting foreign investors is one of the key tasks of privatization. Special attention is focused on portfolio investments of institutional investors, as well as those organized into funds (such as a country fund). To attract active investors, the possibility of a management contract connected with a relatively small shareholding will be considered. The general rule is that these types of investments will have the same fiscal and currency fringe benefits as those of joint ventures. Following the example of other countries, in particular cases of privatization there will be a ceiling placed on foreign investments. Each privatization will be preceded by a procedure of full disclosure and preparation of a prospectus. On the one hand, this should protect the interests of the investor, and on the other it should discredit any charges leveled against giving away state assets, especially to foreign investors.

Capital Markets

As is evident from the above assessments, privatization is not the ultimate goal but rather the means by which an effective and flexible market economy with well-functioning capital markets can be created.

The four basic elements of Polish capital markets can be envisaged as follows.[1]

1. This concept was presented by the author to and accepted by the Economic Committee of the Council of Ministers as guidelines for development of capital markets in Poland.

Types of Securities

From the beginning, different types of securities will exist, as various types of issuers will seek funds using a variety of instruments. The market will initially be dominated by the shares of privatized state-owned companies. This situation will impact on capital markets in three significant areas:

1. The shares will be seen by investors as securities with a specific quality "guarantee."
2. The supply of shares can fluctuate as a result of consecutive privatizations.
3. Prices on the secondary market can drop (compared to the primary market) because of discounted selling to employees.

Another source of shares will be the creation of joint-stock companies on the basis of private local and foreign capital.

Bonds of state-owned and private enterprises will be the next important instrument on the securities market. Enterprises currently are allowed to issue bonds, even though there is neither secondary market for these bonds nor an institutional control of their legality. Within the measure of enterprise budgetary constraints, and more costly bank credit, one has to expect a growing tendency to raise capital through issuing bonds. Newly elected local governments are also likely to use bonds as a source of financing.

The experience of the last two years has shown the innovative power of Polish entrepreneurs, who created new hybrid financial instruments.

Regulatory Framework

Regulatory decisions will be entrusted to the Securities and Exchange Commission, acting on the basis of the Securities Law. The Securities Law will secure investors' interests by specifying procedures for admitting shares to the market, licensing, and monitoring intermediaries.

The Securities Commission, on the basis of the Securities Law, will decide on a public or private offer of stocks and shares. In the case of a public offering of shares and bonds, the criterion for determination is the mandatory registration of the issue with the commission. The registration will be based on data delivered to the commission, and it must include the quantity, type, and method of issue; information on the issuer, including the amount of capital, activities, and previous financial records as determined by the commission; information on management; future plans and forecasts for funds obtained through the issue; and data on the intermediary firm acting as a sponsor.

Intermediaries

Brokerage firms will be licensed and monitored in a continuous manner beginning from the moment that trading of the first shares of private enterprises begins. The following five rules will be the basis of access and activity: (1) passing of an exam; (2) meeting capital requirements; (3) abiding to the norms of behavior toward clients; (4) possessing the appropriate resources necessary for fulfilling the functions of a brokerage firm; and (5) no criminal record in the economic sphere.

Licensing will cover brokerage firms as well as those employed by the firm and having direct contact with the public. The licensing function in the first stage will be fulfilled by the commission. With the development of the market, the powers authorized by the commission in relation to the intermediaries will be delegated to self-governed organizations of intermediaries.

An important role in the brokerage system will be fulfilled by banks. Under the Banking Law, banks can fulfill the function of an intermediary (broker), which does not exempt persons fulfilling the function of a broker and investment adviser in the bank from obtaining a license. From the point of view of the functioning of the market, it would be desirable for banks to create their own, separately capitalized brokerage subsidiaries.

Purchases for the firm's own account will be allowed only in small amounts necessary for liquidity purposes. The activities on the capital market of firms and persons acting simultaneously as brokers and dealers (principals) will be allowed only after the strengthening of the market.

Trading System

In the first years the Stock Exchange will be the only channel of securities trading, which means either a direct transaction on the Exchange or the registration of the transaction by the Exchange. This is justified by the need for an integrated market, specifically in the first stages, when the quantity of transactions, the time period, and the behavior of intermediaries and individual investors are largely unknown. Standardization of the methods of transaction does not indicate uniformity of intermediaries. The Exchange will be open to all licensed brokerage firms and will operate on the basis of concluding a transaction through the matching of bids and offers made by brokers.

The registration of shares and the settlement system of shares transactions will represent the most difficult, the most expensive, and, simultaneously, the most fundamental technical problem for the functioning of the capital market. We support a share registration system based on a computerized central register. This solution avoids an abnormal labor-consuming system of documentation in settlement procedures, price integration of the market, and the systematic control of the market. The central registration does not mean that it is necessary to have individual personal accounts. In this respect it is possible to have a policy whereby the central register of shares consists of either named shares of specific persons (which is rare) or block entries of shares held in the name of the shareholder through specific, licensed intermediaries on the market.

CONCLUSION

The consequences of privatization and the market-driven distribution of capital will go far beyond the economy. Above all, it means abandonment of the ideological paradigm of a "social justice"–driven society that was deeply rooted in public consciousness. An important social condition and designation of privatization is the creation of a middle class, that is, Polish capitalists who would stabilize the democratic changes. Discussion on the privatization law can be treated as an acid test. Three main lines of thinking have emerged during this debate:

1. *Pseudo-Privatization:* A solution based on state-created and state-controlled institutions "playing the market game." This way of thinking can be easily traced to the so-called market socialism proposed by Oscar Lange in the 1930s.
2. *Workers' Self-Management:* Strengthened by self-ownership. As a result, it would give us a mixture of Yugoslavian self-management, West German *mitbestimmung* (seats on a board of directors guaranteed by law for employee representatives), and American employee stock ownership plans.
3. *Individual Ownership:* Following Western patterns but with elements of nineteenth-century idealistic liberalism—that is, the economic role of the government reduced to "night watchman" duties and a free market controlled by individual entrepreneurs and shareholders rather than by the concentrated capital of private and/or institutions such as banks and pensions funds.

For the time being, the third way of thinking has won in the Polish Parliament, but that does not mean that privatization and the introduction of capital market institutions will open an easy road to a free-market society in Poland.

4

The Second Revolution: The Economic Transformation of Poland

Robert L. Konski and Andrew G. Berg

On January 1, 1990, the Polish government began the most radical economic reform ever attempted in modern economic history, transforming a centrally planned economy into a Western-style competitive market economy based on private ownership. At the same time, the government executed a shock stabilization program to choke hyperinflation, which had ballooned to an annual rate of 2000% in the last half of 1989.

The early results are encouraging. The currency has been stabilized and made convertible for all trade transactions, and inflation has slowed dramatically to a current rate of 3 to 4 percent per month, which the government hopes to damp further. The fundamental switch from an economy of shortage to a normal market economy has begun, and the economic environment in which private and state enterprises operate has been radically transformed. For the first time, enterprises cannot automatically sell all they produce, and most shortages have been eliminated. In addition, stabilization and the removal of trade barriers have brought competitive pressures to Poland from the world economy, and the prospects for Poland's export sector are good, as exports are booming.

In July 1990 the legislative branch established the conditions for abolishing a strong pillar of communism—namely, the almost-complete state ownership of the means of production—by agreeing on guidelines for privatizing state enterprises. After three months of heated discussions, the lower house of the Polish Parliament (Sejm) passed on July 13 the privatization bill by a surprising landslide of 328 votes, with 2 opposing votes and 39 abstentions. On July 24, the Senate accepted the Sejm's version of the bill, with 60 senators voting for the bill, 7 against, and 2 abstaining. The president signed the bill shortly after the Senate's approval.

The parliamentary process sent a strong message to observers of the political and economic situation in Poland: Even radically opposed political parties can reach a consensus on issues of this weight and importance.

Despite great strides made in creating the framework for a market economy, the still-dominant state sector of the economy remains weak, a situation that has strained public support for the austerity measures. During the recent presidential elections, calls were made both for acceleration of the transformation and for greater caution. The overwhelming support ultimately given to Lech Walesa, who has indicated his intention to continue the current program, demonstrates the public's determination to see the economic revolution succeed. Continuing low output and further declines in employment in the state sector will, however, tax the patience of the Polish people.

While there are already some signs of recovery, the depth and duration of the recession are unpredictable. The challenge facing the government is to consolidate the fragile stability already achieved, further reduce the inflation rate, and speed up the process of structural adjustment needed if sustainable growth is to be accomplished. Important tasks, such as privatization, demonopolization, banking reforms, tax reforms, the adoption of a modern accounting standard, legal-code reforms, and environmental cleanup, are being undertaken. The government has explained to the population that efforts to artificially stimulate the economy would endanger the stabilization process and thus undermine the achievement of these goals.

This paper briefly describes the economic context facing the new government when it took office in September 1989, discusses the key elements of Poland's economic program, and examines the most important economic problem being tackled by the government: privatization and the various schemes for its implementation.

THE SITUATION IN SEPTEMBER 1989

When the present government took power in September 1989, the Polish economy not only suffered the drawbacks of an Eastern European–type socialist economy but also those of a market economy out of macroeconomic control. The economic system was based neither on the plan nor the market. About half of all prices were free, but many scarce resources remained under administrative control. The price system was in disarray, with many key relative prices, such as the price of energy, wildly out of line. International trade was subject to pervasive restrictions, while foreign exchange was rationed, almost isolating the economy completely from foreign competition. Most restrictions on the private sector had been lifted in 1989, but monopolistic public enterprises, which had dominated the economy for decades, were still accustomed to cheap bank credits, excess demand for their outputs, and lack of competition.

The progress made by the previous government in moving toward a market economy did not prevent a rapid deterioration of the economic situation. The absence of adequate controls over monetary, fiscal, or wage policy, combined with a sharp rise in food prices resulting from sweeping food-price liberalization, fueled hyperinflation. The ballooning budget deficit was financed primarily by the printing of money. As inflation accelerated, tax revenues, public utility charges, and energy prices fell behind, exacerbating the budget deficit. In the face of this intolerable situation, the new government decided not to try to live with inflation, believing such a course would preclude all efforts at structural adjustment. Instead, the government attempted to halt inflation with a comprehensive stabilization program designed to combine tight macroeconomic control with the liberalization of prices and foreign trade.[1]

1. See Chapter 3 by Gregory Jedrzejczak in this volume for a discussion of government strategy and program results.

RESTRUCTURING PRIVATIZATION

Objective of Privatization

The Polish economic reform is currently at a critical juncture. The first stage of the reform—the fight against inflation—has been fairly successful, but the reform has not yet succeeded in achieving the far-reaching restructuring of the Polish economy that is crucial to improving the long-term economic prospects of the country. There has been, as yet, only very limited privatization activity in Eastern Europe, where the state as owner of an enterprise sells an existing stake or permits its ownership to be diluted through recapitalization. Privatization in post-socialist economies represents a completely unprecedented challenge. The goals of this challenge are to privatize thousands of state-owned enterprises, representing the majority of Poland's industrial base, and to achieve levels of state ownership encountered in Western Europe. The government would like to accomplish this task as quickly as possible; it hopes to find, over the next few years, owners for enterprises producing at least 60 percent of the gross domestic product.

Results Expected from Privatization

What does the government expect from rapid privatization? Speed is a crucial element of a proposed privatization program. The inefficient enterprise system is hampering stabilization and economic growth. The government is accountable for the inability of the state-owned enterprises to restructure, and their failure to ignite economic growth is blamed on the government. Wide-scale privatization would help Poland in the following ways:

1. by creating an environment in which a true market economy could thrive;
2. by establishing and developing capital markets, so that financial resources could be mobilized for efficient uses and information could be gathered about firms;
3. by creating the legal structure of a corporate economy, so that firms have owners to whom management is responsible, and

so that the basic state economic role is regulation and monitoring, not direct control;

4. by providing employees a fair, but not dominant, opportunity to participate in ownership;

5. by spreading the ownership of enterprises to as large as possible a segment of the population;

6. by instilling financial and market discipline in enterprise managers;

7. by reducing the social costs of the transformation; and

8. by creating opportunities for and encouraging foreign capital to invest, thus stimulating the inflow of Western technology, managerial skills, and know-how.

Obstacles to the Privatization Process

The government has come up against several obstacles that could hinder privatization efforts.

1. *Lack of Capital:* This lowers the prices at which enterprises can be sold, opening the way for foreigners and those few Poles with large amounts of liquid assets to buy up the bulk of the available shares cheaply. This, in turn, might generate popular resentment and prevent privatization from developing political support. If enterprises are valued at high prices, the market for their shares may be stagnant. If they are valued too low, public outcry and criticism is likely.

2. *Lack of Infrastructure:* A financial and organizational infrastructure to carry out the privatization on a mass scale is missing and must be built effectively from the ground up. In addition, there is a weak overall physical and services environment, including a lack of appropriate telecommunications, banks, and other specialized services.

3. *Lack of Cadres:* Poland simply does not have enough people with the appropriate skills, experience, and business culture to carry out a privatization program on the scale it would like. There are no active investors to speak of, and the capacities in the field of valuing privatizing companies, for example, are very limited.

4. *Lack of a Model to Follow:* There are no examples of privatization
   on the scale remotely comparable to that planned for Poland.
   Consequently, solutions and approaches utilized in other countries that have been through the process are not easy to trans-
   pose onto Polish soil. Some 7,000 significant state-owned enterprises are being considered for privatization in Poland. In
   contrast, between 1980 and 1987, the Decade of Privatization,
   600 firms were privatized throughout the world.

Groundwork for Privatization

There have been substantial accomplishments in preparing the
proper environment for privatization. The preparation of the necessary legislative framework is one such prerequisite. Recent legislative changes have revived the freedom of economic and trade activity. There are three legal principles relevant to economic activity:

1. *The Principle of Freedom:* Every entity can conduct economic activity. This ended the virtually monopolistic dogma of the previous regime, which stated that any and all economic activity
   should be organized and carried out by the state, with exceptions allowed for by explicit written consent.
2. *The Principle of Equality:* All economic entities are equal
   whether they are state, private, or cooperative in nature. Even
   further, the "sectoral" differentiation of enterprises is to be
   eliminated in the near future.
3. *The Principle of Legality:* All activities of economic entities are to
   be conducted with full accordance to the law.

The Law on Economic Activity eliminated the hiring and size
limits imposed on private enterprises. It also eliminated private
enterprises' obligation to participate in professional organizations
through which they were "plugged" into the planning of the
economy.

Among other crucial laws paving the way to privatization is an
updated bankruptcy law, which in its latest version allows for a
state enterprise to be liquidated via bankruptcy. So far, no enter-

prise has been declared formally bankrupt, as neither banks nor fellow enterprises have been willing to initiate bankruptcy proceedings. The government itself will have to take action against several enterprises that are in arrears to it. To prevent mismanagement of resources and haste in the process of liquidation, distressed but potentially viable enterprises will be evaluated and, where advisable, helped by the Agency for Industrial Restructuring.

A new banking law is being prepared with the help of international organizations such as the World Bank. Several Western banks have entered the Polish market under the existing conditions, and more applications for permits to start operations in Poland are pending.

The government is completing preparation for a reform of the fiscal system, which will include the introduction of a uniform corporate income tax for all economic entities, a broad-based personal income tax, and replacement of the sales tax by a value-added tax by the beginning of 1992 at the latest.

Privatization Methods

There are many different approaches proposed for the privatization of Poland's state-owned enterprises; indeed, opinions sometimes seem to outnumber experts in the field. No existing blueprints of privatization could adequately fit Poland's needs. Some general principles, however, are fairly clear.

1. Traditional case-by-case methods will be prohibitively slow. Techniques such as public-tender offers of shares at a set price require that each firm be carefully analyzed, valued, and perhaps restructured prior to privatization. The record from other countries suggests that even in the best of circumstances privatizing anything close to the thousands of companies required would take decades. Poland faces unusual difficulties compared to other countries with extensive experience in privatization, as it suffers from a lack of cadres, financial infrastructure, and experience with markets. Finally, each privatization will pose a unique problem requiring negotiations with workers, potential

buyers, and so on. A single major failure could derail the process.

2. The current state of affairs is very dangerous. While the state maintains ultimate ownership of state enterprises, control over assets and management is weak and ambiguous and is shared among central government, management, and workers. What this means in practice is that resistance to wage demands must come from the central government itself, not management, that no one inside the firm has a clear interest in seeing that any sale of assets takes place at an appropriate price, and that decisions about investment and use of current assets will tend to neglect long-term considerations.

3. The problem is essentially one of how to transfer ownership to private hands in a way that satisfies the goals outlined above. Several pieces of the solution have been offered:

   a. An obvious answer is simply to give shares directly to each citizen. While this turns out to be administratively extremely difficult, it does not, more importantly, establish adequate control over management, at least in the medium term. No single owner or small group of owners would have a large enough stake to encourage them to expend the necessary effort to monitor management. The concentration of shares through secondary-market trades could take many years.

   b. Consequently, some sort of financial intermediation will probably play a part. A financial intermediary is simply an institution—for example, a bank, mutual fund, or pension fund—that holds and manages financial assets for its own owners. The idea would be to distribute shares of former state enterprises to such intermediaries. Ownership in these intermediaries can be transferred to the public in many ways. For example, shares in mutual funds could be distributed to the population, or each bank could sell individually through traditional methods.

   These intermediaries should be designed so that normal market-control mechanisms that help discipline such institutions in the West can function. These include, for example, incentive contracts for managers based on the market value of the shares in the intermediary itself or of the underlying portfolio. Clearly, it will be a challenge to create the environment in which such institutions can function well. Foreign participation in the management of these institutions will help. Finally, even in the West it is often felt that such financial institutions are inferior to direct private ownership of corporations in encouraging good management performance. Thus in many schemes these intermediaries are designed to play a temporary role.

c. Many schemes that involve the distribution to the population of some sort of special money that could be used only to buy assets from the state have been called "voucher" proposals. The aim is to solve some of the distributional problems of selling state assets when much of the population has meager financial resources, and when those who have money may be assumed to have come by it unfairly. Such schemes have the potential advantage of allowing mass active participation in privatization. For some of the same reasons that direct distribution is problematic, vouchers will have to be used in combination with other methods, in particular intermediation. For example, they could be used to purchase shares of financial intermediaries like mutual funds, which in turn would use the vouchers to get shares from the government.

4. In the meantime, "commercialization," the conversion of state enterprises to the corporate form, will be necessary. Policymakers are justifiably skeptical about schemes to reform the public sector and to make it behave like private firms without privatization; indeed, decades of experiments have convinced them that this is a futile endeavor. It is vital, however, to establish ownership rights and clarify legal responsibilities as soon as possible, for, as mentioned above, the current situation is precarious. The establishment of the corporate form alone, with a board of directors representing the government as shareholder and management directly responsible to this board of directors, is no substitute for privatization. It is an important final step, however, as it paves the way for sale of shares and more generally establishes that the corporation will be the dominant organizational form for large enterprises.

5. Any solution will be a combination of methods. Rapid commercialization of a large number of enterprises will get the process going. Some of the shares will be given or sold cheaply to workers. Some will be distributed to intermediaries. Some may be sold or distributed to the public directly, perhaps through vouchers.

CONCLUSION

The political pressure associated with the process of privatization in Central Europe is perhaps more important than in other countries. There will be resentment against concentration of capital and against exploitation by new owners, especially foreign, unless the process of privatization is coupled with a successful public relations campaign. There is an existing fear that the inadequacy of domestic resources will lead to excessive foreign control. Excessive foreign ownership is not yet a problem; on the contrary, the government currently is more concerned with attracting foreign investment and creating the proper business culture. In fact, substantial foreign investment is hoped for as a means of bringing new capital, managerial skills, and technology to Poland.

Poland's privatization program has many goals. The keys, however, are few. The program must clearly establish that Poland will have a private corporate economy, and that there will be no attempt to find an illusory "third way" between central planning and Western-type market economies. The program must move rapidly in this direction, as domestic and foreign management, expertise, and capital must be mobilized for the comprehensive restructuring that needs to take place.

The program must be socially acceptable. It should involve as many as possible in the process of structural reforms and generate a broad new class of owners that is not dominated by the old favored group, the *nomenklatura*. The route taken in Great Britain and emulated elsewhere is a necessary part of privatization, but clearly it will not be enough. In fact, all traditional methods (for example, public offerings and private placement) are too slow for a project of this magnitude. Creative solutions must and will be found.

5

Where We Are Headed: The Case of Czechoslovakia

Michal Mejstrik

Czechoslovakia must take radical measures to restructure its industry in order to meet world standards, but the country faces a very hostile environment for the reintroduction of a market structure. Economic reformers face a market dominated by large state monopolies, which were created and maintained by administrative action rather than economic determination. That market almost completely lacks a private sector, even when compared to Hungary or Poland.

A "coalition structure," made possible by collusive behavior among officials in still-existing, often artificial monopolies and oligopolies, has its own system of barter exchange and an informal network of input distribution, where prices play a secondary role. The trump card in an exchange is the ability to deliver special "deficit" products, such as industrial materials in short supply, certain consumer goods, or even a bonus system of vacations.

The traditional assumption of top-down planning is largely a fallacy. The collusion of formal and informal interest groups creates an illusion of "plan struggle," so often depicted by Western analysts of centrally planned economies (CPEs). In reality, the collusive oligopoly decides on a distribution of resources and benefits primarily for the internal rewards of the "Mafia."[1]

This coalition structure is deeply rooted in its informal nature, where behavioral patterns cannot be easily changed, despite the

1. This concept was originally discussed by Mlcoch Lubos, published officially (1989) and unofficially between 1980 and 1983.

transformation to a market-based economy. As already shown over the last decade in Yugoslavia, Hungary, and Poland, partial reforms of cuts in state subsidies and liberalization of prices of certain product groups can help to create an environment more conducive to a market structure. However, these partial reforms can also lead to a system of mutual lending and subsidization within the coalition, which in turn creates new problems.

The principal starting point for reform is the full or partial privatization of state firms, as well as the development of a new private sector of small and medium-sized firms. The former process would be prefaced by the breakup of the monopolies and/or the internal decentralization of management decisionmaking, in hopes of easing the rigid and highly centralized nature of the internal organization of state firms.

However, the formal breakup of these enterprises will not necessarily dissolve the coalition structure. In fact, in such a small, closed economy as that of Czechoslovakia, the individual units of former state firms would become monopolies in their own right. Thus, Czechoslovakia is faced with the monumental task of creating basic competition—that is, alternative suppliers who offer alternative selections of prices and qualities of goods.

Renewing the dynamism of Czechoslovakia's prewar market economy has to be achieved in the context of a globalized economy, which has already transformed some industries into independent multinational entities. Perhaps the greatest barrier to the transition of Czechoslovakia to a market economy, according to some independent observers, is a public attitude still rooted in the idea of a nation-state. Another barrier may be the unwillingness of people to sacrifice their high standard of living during a reform period that imposes austerity on the economy. However, on the positive side, Czechoslovakia has a low level of foreign debt and negligible inflation, which make its economy considerably healthier in some respects than its Eastern European neighbors.

The proposed changes in the macroeconomic and institutional framework should create a hospitable environment for a transition to a competitive market. The final transition program should be comprehensive, seeking to minimize the transition period and adjustment costs. The main controversy in Czechoslovakia has been between gradualists and radicals over the speed, depth, and tools of this process. Some external factors (for example, reduced oil supplies and oil price increases) accelerated public discussion in the direction of the radical reform package, adopted by the federal government in May 1990. The interim National Assembly passed dozens of important new laws during the spring. Later in the year the newly elected National Assembly (a different group from the interim) was able to elaborate and pass the blueprint of radical transition that introduced a number of simultaneous major measures as of January 1, 1991.

The Czechoslovak adjustment process is closely supervised by International Monetary Fund (IMF) and World Bank experts, who facilitated Czechoslovakia's reentry into both economic organizations while providing the country with valuable independent expertise. Because it is in Central Europe, Czechoslovakia primarily follows European Community (EC) patterns of economic and legal organization in order to be prepared for its affiliation with the EC.

THE NEW MACROECONOMIC FRAMEWORK

A heated debate has arisen between proponents of expansionary policy combined with gradual structural transformation and proponents of restrictive fiscal and monetary policy. The former represent a certain form of the populism paradigm (see Dornbusch and Edwards 1990) that emphasizes growth, "fair and just" prices, taxes, and exchange rates that reflect a somewhat egalitarian income distribution. This approach also deemphasizes the risk that inflation and deficit finance may be side effects of expansionary policies. The proponents of restrictive fiscal and monetary anti-inflationary policy, represented by Federal Finance Minister Vaclav Klaus, stress the need for a surplus budget, flat taxes, equilibrium prices, wages, and exchange rate. In turn, they emphasize the risk and negative impact of inflation. As a necessary complement, they see radical supply-side recommendations involving the promotion of new private establishments and rapid privatization. Of course, suggested anti-inflationary tools liquidate traditional growth instruments used by centrally planned economies and slow economic growth.

In fact, both groups have a common point of departure—preservation of the favorable initial conditions for Czechoslovak transformation—but they differ in their recommendations of what policies to pursue once the traditional systems of central planning collapse. One easily can see that the federal government is trying to avoid the mistakes of Poland and Hungary—which led to inflation and ineffective foreign borrowing—and to follow successful Czechoslovak adjustments after World War I under the policy of Finance Minister Alois Rasin, who succeeded in preventing hyperinflation and indebtedness.

The current reform program was initially strongly influenced by restrictive budget and monetary policy. The "tight" money policy of the relatively independent state bank consists of limiting money supply growth targets (currently 3 percent), allowing only 1 to 2 percent growth of credits for 1990 and gradually increasing the discount rate (from 4 to 5 percent in 1990 to 8.5 percent in 1991). The main goals of monetary policy in a stormy reform period are to keep internal purchasing power of the currency and its foreign exchange rate stable, to equilibrate the balance of payments, and to promote banking-sector development (for example, the reintroduction of mortgage institutions). Now the actual interest rate can be higher than the discount rate by 14.5 percent (for the beginning of 1991) on short-term (one-year) credits, 3 percent on middle-term (four-year) credits, 4 percent on long-term (ten-year) credits, and 8 percent on overnight credits. Since inflation growth has been slow, real interest rates are positive. No new soft working capital credits are provided to finance inventory. Interest rates for such forms of financing remain steady at 6 percent, while these special credits are gradually converted into standard loans. These credits have been "quasicredits," and they financially covered the permanent necessity of these inventories. Firms have never been forced to repay these credits, nor have they been stimulated to create firms' deposits. A growing number of firms have their own foreign exchange accounts at commercial banks.

Recently established state-owned commercial banks are regulated by the state bank through money supply, the discount rate, 5 percent reserve requirements of total deposits, and by government control of the national increase of indebtedness in convertible currencies and rules of foreign exchange liquidity (for example, decreasing the share of liabilities against some less developed countries, which are quite illiquid). In fact, the banking infrastructure is underdeveloped; it has been called the museum of financial instruments. Czechoslovakia's sixteen established banks are weak and require foreign assistance. A growing number of foreign banks have opened representative offices in Czechoslovakia, and some of them have shown interest in investing in joint-venture banks. State-owned commercial banks should be transformed into joint-stock companies, as I discuss in a later section.

Nevertheless, people can now also consider investments in bonds or shares that have been issued experimentally in limited amounts by Czechoslovak economic agents and can be bought only by Czechoslovak organizations and citizens. Foreigners are not allowed to take part in this trade. Relevant legislation should be passed by the end of 1990, and the Prague Stock Exchange will eventually open.

On the fiscal side, to reach the surplus budget the government slashed spending in areas such as defense and culture and also made deep cuts in passive subsidies used to cover enterprise losses. Subsidies and cuts in agriculture were combined in the budget with compensatory price increases (see below). One can expect strong lobbying in favor of higher subsidies and lower taxes. Proposed tax reform tied in with restricted government spending should allow both enterprise and personal taxes to be lowered from the present 60 percent to 40–50 percent of GNP.

The changes in relative prices through price and trade liberalization will inevitably bring some moderate inflationary pressures. Here the role of monetary and fiscal policy is to alleviate rather than accelerate those pressures, even at the cost of slowing growth.

THE NEW MICROECONOMIC AND
INSTITUTIONAL FRAMEWORK

Following the tradition of Joseph Alois Schumpeter, we see dynamic entrepreneurs and dynamic competition as driving forces of economic development. It is the role of the entrepreneur to create innovations and to destroy old equilibria by establishing new com-

binations (Hanusch 1990). Along with the process of "creative de-
struction," progress in total factor productivity and product innovation will be achieved. In addition, dynamic competition, forced by
innovations, provides the necessary transfer of productivity gains to
the consumer, resulting in an increase in social welfare.

To achieve a dynamic market environment, Czechoslovakia must
go through radical institutional adjustments. The basic legislative
measures lie in separating the political and economic power of the
state and in separating public and private law. Among the several
dozen interim acts passed in the spring and autumn National
Assembly are an amended business code and laws on joint ventures, small privatization, restitution of nationalized assets, and
foreign exchange. Redistribution of the competence of central
agencies was accelerated by national tensions that came mainly
from Slovakia. There is now a tendency to organize economic life
mainly in the autonomous Czech and Slovak republics within the
federation. The federal Czech and Slovak budgets will rely on
clearly specified fractions of total tax revenues. Specific government
agencies should be created then, such as an internal revenue bureau with local branches and a bureau for antitrust policy. The related costs ought to be covered by cuts from the existing bureaucracy
of the central planning system.

The Liberalization of Prices and the
Introduction of Limited Convertibility

A major step in moving toward the market system lies in renewing the role of prices. The command economy saw prices as an
often manipulated instrument of evidence based on individual firm
costs and agreed markup supplemented by individual subsidies. To
liberalize prices in a highly monopolized, small economy, as in
Czechoslovakia, could harm the important macroeconomic objective
of ensuring stable prices within free markets. Only if free markets are to be renewed simultaneously can prices and quantities be
determined by the market forces of supply and demand, to the
maximum possible extent that allows the economy to allocate resources efficiently and in a way that is responsive to individual
tastes. The promotion of the development of the domestic private

sector combined with competitive imports should help to create a sufficient competitive environment accompanied by restrictive macroeconomic policy. These major measures might be successful only as a simultaneous package. Of course, the prerequisite for import competition is a convertible currency. Note that in a gradualist's opinion, one should postpone it and liberalize according to the sequential creation of a competitive market.

As a step toward price liberalization, price subsidies to agricultural products were eliminated as of July 10, 1990. The maximum price increase was combined with an egalitarian 100 percent wage compensation. Demand fell sharply, and, as a welcome response of producers, the actual equilibrium prices of some products fell below the maximum prices. Thus, for the first time in today's Czechoslovakia, the consumers beat the producers.

Meanwhile, the removal of subsidies and a retail price hike of up to 20 percent are expected for other areas, such as fuel, transportation tariffs, and housing rental. Simultaneously, a unification of individual sales tax rates should occur as a point of departure for the interconnection of separated retail and wholesale prices. The lowering of the highest sales taxes provides a specific kind of compensation. The deep change of the tax system should put it closer to EC standards by adoption of a value-added tax, an income tax, and a corporation tax by January 1, 1993.

The liberalization of goods and services prices with a slightly adjusted tax system should come into effect on January 1, 1991, together with further liberalization of imports and exports promoted by limited exchange-rate convertibility.[2] A temporary cushion of this operation should be provided by the reintroduction of general import tariffs and firm subsidies. The tariffs and subsidies should be lowered, step by step, to allow for real free-trade conditions.

The liberalization of imports and exports proceeds under conditions of a rapidly changing territorial structure of trade in favor of the West, and it cannot successfully be achieved without some form of currency convertibility. The existing system of originally individualized foreign exchange retention quotas (in 1990 70 percent for all firms) has led to the step-by-step dollarization of the

---

2. The government will maintain greater control over prices of transport, public utilities, health care, and oil products.

Czechoslovak economy, where the medium of exchange between the domestic and foreign markets (dollar, deutsche mark) is more important than the medium of exchange used by domestic market agents (korun).   The interconnection of foreign and domestic markets should be smoothed by overnight introduction of limited convertibility for the koruna (internal convertibility), that is, liberalization of current-account transactions for domestic residents. The foreign currency accounts of the firms should be cancelled. Hard currency revenues are to be deposited in the banks and converted into koruna accounts at the going exchange rate. Proposed forced conversion should be accompanied by the possibility of resident firms to buy necessary amounts of convertible currency at current market rates for commercial imports.   Even if the control of capital flow is kept, this solution opens the problem of capital flight through the underinvoicing of exports and the overinvoicing of imports.   Latin American experience shows that firms retain the part of their deposits abroad in order to avoid forced conversion.   In any case, even such a half-way measure to convertibility will be guaranteed by standby credits of US$2 billion from international financial institutions to keep the rate of exchange as stable as possible.

Government officials are now trying to determine the korun's initial foreign exchange rate.   Until October 1990 the official exchange rate for most transactions was around 16.6 koruna per dollar, significantly lower than the tourist rate (around 25 koruna per dollar) and foreign exchange auctions rate (around 33 koruna per dollar).   Firms originally used these foreign exchange auctions as a way of protecting some parts of profits from heavy taxation (75 percent) and to use the bought currency as a cost of imports. Meanwhile, the black-market tourist rate is not too high.   As a result, the initial level of foreign exchange is likely to be a devaluation of around 56 percent, to 24 koruna per dollar, which could cause some additional inflationary pressures that should be captured by complementary measures from the reform basket (such as anti-inflationary policy or import competition).   There will be necessary social costs in closing enterprises and subsequent unemployment.   These costs should be foreseen and social policy adjustments made quickly.

The Commercialization and Privatization of
State-Owned Enterprises

In Czechoslovakia more than 97 percent of the net material product (NMP) is produced by the "socialist sector."[3] Besides cooperatives (nearly 10 percent of NMP), the contribution of state-owned enterprises (SOEs) accounted for nearly 88 percent of NMP. Because of falling efficiency and the informal power structures previously mentioned, step-by-step privatization of SOEs is widely accepted as the inevitable way to surmount many related difficulties and to improve the units' operating efficiency.

The reappraisal of the long-standing tradition of the prevailing state sector and its transformation is, however, still a source of controversy. The reformers, whose ideas were formulated in the 1960s, favor postponing it; indeed, the 1960s reform process did not recognize its importance at all. The radicals suggest speeding it up and minimizing the privatization period for some SOEs at the very least. The main argument here is that one cannot renew a market economy without renewing private ownership. The main purpose of privatization is to create individual fields for sovereign rule by the owner (and exclusion of interference by others, especially government, except for generally recognized duties, such as taxes). Neither the frontiers nor the owners has been well defined, and this ambiguity has been generating an economic and ecological irresponsibility and nontransparent financial relations.

The goals of the privatization process are to substantially decrease the state sector (state-owned assets) and to widen the degree of private ownership among citizens. Property rights should be transferred from government to a broad constituency of individual shareholders. Also, this broad Czechoslovak constituency includes potential critics of privatization, including managers and employees of SOEs and the users of their output. Thus these future shareholders are becoming personally interested and involved in the privatization and are becoming the basis for a powerful political constituency supporting privatization and opposing renationalization. Now there are newly created ministries for privatization and

---

3. NMP is analogous to net national product used in CPEs. It covers only production and excludes services.

property management on a republic level (Czech and Slovak) and a Coordinating Bureau for Privatization and Property Management of the Federal Ministry of Finance, which is responsible for the direct transfer of property when it requires parliamentary approval. According to the Federal Ministry of Finance, perhaps 70 percent of the SOEs are now seen as the subject of privatization.

National property is classified under three categories: Category A consists of public utilities and other regulated SOEs (which are often in public hands and strongly regulated in market economies), and Category B represents state-owned firms that are due to be privatized. Category C refers to municipal property subject to privatization by local governments. The production of public goods and services on federal, republic, and local levels will amount to about three-tenths of the SOEs' share of NMP. The redefining of public goods on the federal level (defense, foreign service), on the republic level (some public utilities), and on the municipal level (collective goods of local importance) should predetermine the nature of federal, republic, and local budgets and their revenues.

Phase 1. Commercialization and Municipalization

The SOEs not producing public goods should be cut from the budget and transformed into joint-stock companies during the last quarter of 1990. Simultaneously, the property claims of the original owners should be considered step by step.

Category B will capture state-owned "heavy industry" (B1) and "light industry" (B2) firms that are due to be privatized. As a necessary precondition (and to allow for divisibility of SOE assets), both subcategories of firms first will be converted into the form of the state-owned corporations (joint-stock companies), with a board of directors appointed by the government. These corporations will be asked to be self-financing, even if it is still possible that informal channels to the government will enable them to acquire tax exceptions or subsidies.

Category C covers newly defined municipal property (municipalization of national property) subject to commercialization and privatization by autonomous local governments. Examples are restaurants, local services, and rental flats, which can be returned to the original property owners (if they produce their claims under the restitution law requirements until 1991) or sold through auctions.

The related costs and revenues of commercialization and privatization will be settled by means of the Fund of National Property, which will also help to settle liabilities of privatized firms.

Phase 2. Privatization

In the short run, Category B1 state-owned corporations will not be privatized right away, though their assets can be temporarily rented and they can enter into joint ventures with foreign participation.

The municipal property of Category C will not, inevitably, be converted into joint-stock companies, but it might be offered directly to the original property owners or to single proprietors as soon as possible (after November local elections).

The state-owned corporations of Category B2 should be the subject of large privatization. How and to whom the equity shares of these corporations will be offered is still being debated.

Optional Models for B2 Privatization

Privatization in Czechoslovakia is hindered by the fact that there is no clear way yet to determine the market value of firms, and that a relatively low level of domestic private savings makes it difficult for the public to buy newly issued shares. Domestic savings total around 330 billion koruna, which represents about one-half of GNP (or about 10 percent of the book value of state assets), and thus are quite insufficient for the purchase of state property (but fairly sufficient to destabilize the domestic market in case of the loss of policy credibility). Further, more than one-third of personal savings is guessed to be in the hands of 5 percent of the citizens, primarily the previous establishment and the participants of the shadow market. The public is unwilling to support the government in giving economic and political power to these people. The current effort to sell off to the first foreign company is often seen as a politically unacceptable form of spontaneous privatization, one that can provide existing managers, often Communist Party functionaries, huge monetary windfalls after selling out at low prices. The experience of Hungary shows that the effort to reverse the prepared agreements with foreign investors could mean the loss of government credibility abroad.

The rationale behind a low price for firms stems from the fact that evaluations of existing firms are based exclusively on a book value (which usually includes extremely low land prices). The author performed several capital asset evaluations that show that the book value of a structure located near the Czech–West German border is nominally the same for a Czech structure in koruna terms (about 3,800 koruna per cubic meter of Czech structure) as for a West German structure in deutsche marks (approximately 3,000 DM per cubic meter of West German structure). The market value of the firm, seen as an initial fixed-price offer might, of course, be equal to zero or might be many times greater than the book value if assets are useful (especially for internationally competitive firms). To assess the market value of a firm from expected cash flows on the basis of distorted product and input prices (based on domestic individual costs and markup combined with nontransparent subsidies) is somewhat naive. Thus, the modifications of common evaluation procedures are required case by case to indicate potential (international) competitiveness or bankruptcy of the firm. Nevertheless, under existing conditions of trade expressed in book value, the employees are often afraid of foreign buyout, particularly if foreigners get rid of useless assets and cut back on labor.

The cross-ownership model of privatization (based on closely linked networks of suppliers and creditors) was widely used in Japan and West Germany after World War II, but it has resulted in many efficiency problems in Hungary and Yugoslavia and is not recommended.

For the beginning of rapid privatization of B2, the Federal Ministry of Finance has recommended and elaborated the unconventional "voucher" model. Under this model, Category B2 enterprises will have marketable shares and 20 to 100 percent of equity would be available for voucher sale. Each citizen would get the same quantity of vouchers—investment money with limited maturity—from the government free of charge. The vouchers would entitle citizens to bid for shares of SOEs. Voucher owners can "buy" some shares at the Dutch auctions that would be conducted for B2 corporations' offered stock. The auctions will be held for a limited period, after which the vouchers will expire. With respect to the lack of citizens' information on offered shares, the system will likely be refined by investment organizations, including holding companies and voucher-market mutual funds (Svejnar 1989, note 7), which would allow concentration of information. Besides the rapid redistribution of property rights, the absent capital market could be created instantly. Neither the state treasury nor the companies receive any financial funds from the investors. However, the state treasury and companies could use the following privatization steps to obtain the funds. As a result of voucher privatization, there will be a group of private owners supervising the firms' management and development.

A suggested model of vouchers exchanged for shares of privatized enterprises represents radical transfer of the ownership rights to individuals, which will further limit budget revenues but should widen the personal income by the dividend. The proposed government-regulated delay of dividend payments by two years would seriously harm the entrepreneurial interests of new shareholders. More reasonable would be similar administrative regulations for new shareholders to allow trading with marketable shares with only a slight delay. It is mostly believed that the market mechanism will force citizens to generate additional pension and social security funds, and that they will behave as responsible investors and not convert their capital (shares or derived options) into liquid money.

The original voucher blueprint of the Federal Ministry of Finance has suggested selling residual shares to domestic and foreign investors, in turn. To compensate for the differentiation between shares given away and shares paid by investors, one might divide the common shares into various classes, offering different voting rights. The open question is how many shares will be available for the public. Then, in conditions of insufficient private, domestic savings, the author would prefer a simultaneous combination of some form of leveraged buyout or leasing in the form of, for example, manager and employee stock ownership plans (ESOPs), consumer stock ownership plans (CSOPs), and general stock ownership corporations (GSOCs), with foreign private capital (through joint ventures with foreign direct investment). The supply of new capital, technology, organization, and management through foreign direct investment is quite necessary for the encouragement of competition and economic growth. Foreign investors should be entitled to buy simultaneously at least part of existing or newly issued shares in an agreed-upon ratio.

Some 10 percent of stocks could be privatized by ESOPs (or related ownership plans) with the government as a lender and the bank as a trust. The repayment of employee stocks by dividends can provide:

1. stable revenue flows for the government that can be used in the future—for example, for repayments to original property owners;
2. incentives for workers to limit strikes and other forms of industrial conflict, as well as to push for wage growth. The author agrees with Svejnar (1989) that these factors would be important components of a successful transition program and would support anti-inflationary policy from the microeconomic level. To enforce it, employees could buy exclusively or partially the preferred stocks that have either conditional voting rights or none at all. As the households have regular income expectations from normal growth of wages, which they augment by expected future earnings from equity holdings, they will probably raise their savings to agree with the higher discounted stream of anticipated receipts. Even if they claim only moderate wage increases, they will not have to consume less if the scheme stimulates investment and shifts the growth path;
3. ESOPs the opportunity to increase the quality of goods and to decrease the costs (Conte and Svejnar 1990); and
4. an exogenous increase in the price of (employee) stocks of the firm, because employee stockholders would be deeply interested in foreign direct investment.

The debate on the privatization models might reach the conclusion: Let all flowers grow. However, new private establishments have been absent in our treatment of the private sector so far (McDermott and Mejstrik 1990).

FOREIGN INVESTMENT

Czechoslovakia's trade picture has begun to reflect recent changes, both at home and abroad. The low-quality machinery and defense industry exports to developing and Eastern European countries have declined, thanks to limited availability of credits for those sometimes illiquid countries. Hand in hand with the transformation of Czechoslovakia, new markets are opening; examples of this include new trade and cooperation treaties with the EC and the United States. The flexibility of exporters increased when a monopoly of fifty state-owned trading companies was dismantled. About 1,000 firms have already been authorized to conduct foreign trade activities. (Foreign trade was fully liberalized for all firms on January 1, 1990). The ministry bureaucrats still limit convertible exports and imports of some items through cumbersome licensing. Mainly exports of raw materials and semimanufactured goods are the subject of licensing, which might alleviate the effects of distorted domestic prices still separated from the world market. The export and import licenses and quotas should be substituted by more effective tariff adjustments or general technical and ecological standards.

Czechoslovakia's low level of foreign debt, now US$8 billion, can be easily managed (with 20 percent of exports going toward servicing the debt), and the balance of payments is not in the red; the country is, in fact, a net creditor to developed and developing market economies. The difficult reorientation of trade from East to West should rely on much better market research rather than passive adjustment at the cost of indebtedness. Only reasonable standby and other loans can facilitate the smooth adjustment.

Foreign investors could play an important role in this process. The stable Czechoslovak economy allows it to "go East," because large Eastern European markets and especially Russian markets are well understood by Czech and Slovak business leaders, who usually speak Russian, or to "go West," an opportunity considered primarily by the Japanese, who take into account Eastern Europe's relatively skilled labor and low transport costs, among other factors.

The relevant legislation is being adopted step by step. One obvious obstacle is risk aversion—wherein a certain part of the Czechoslovak population is afraid of being fired by foreign owners—but domestic demand for additional convertible investment is high. Even more important than the reliable supplies of high-technology or innovative products, it seems to be an up-to-date (imported or transferred) organization and management, allowing for domestic firms to restructure with respect to unknown standards of Western markets and marketing techniques.

The important steps in the right direction are represented by legislation regarding foreign direct investment and relevant bilateral agreements on foreign direct investment protection and profit repatriation. The simplest case could come when the company is 100 percent foreign-owned. Foreign investors who want to set up joint ventures must receive approval from the Ministry of Finance, which assesses the financial soundness of the proposed investment project from domestic and foreign points of view. Currently, investors are required to convert 30 percent of convertible currency revenues into koruna. Importers producing for domestic markets without sufficient exports can obtain convertible currency at foreign exchange auctions. The "limited convertibility" introduced January 1, 1991, should clear the situation. Under bilateral investment protection agreements (BIPs), repatriated profits transferred abroad now are free and guaranteed by the government. There is local currency financing available for joint ventures. A minimum of 5 percent of gross profits is required to contribute into a single reserve fund that must be maintained at a minimum of 10 percent of the joint venture's basic capital. Separate social security funds of the firms' contributions are the same as domestic firms', amounting to 50 percent of the payroll. There are tax deductions provided for the joint ventures, as they pay profit tax at 40 percent (compared to a tax rate of 50 percent for state enterprises and 60 percent for foreign-trade corporations), and dividends are usually taxed at 25 percent.

The main problem for joint ventures reflects unresolved privatization issues. Before acquiring an asset of the SOE or other state property by joint-venture means, one must address its partial or full privatization and its partial or full participation of foreign investors. Can this obstacle be overcome? As supposed in the interim solution, large enterprises should also be approved by the government, and only a minority of SOE assets should participate in the joint venture. The capital asset evaluation, however, is a problem in itself. The claims of former property owners whose holdings were expropriated in the past should be respected in some manner. The final solution of foreign direct investment questions related to privatization is the subject of the National Assembly, but the establishment of joint ventures in the suggested restricted form should be initiated immediately. Proposed full privatization will widen possibilities further.

REFERENCES

Bulír, Ales. 1990. *The Banking System in Czechoslovakia VP*. Prague: Institute of Economic Sciences.

Conte, Michael, and Jan Svejnar. 1990. "The Performance Effect of Employee Ownership Plans." In *Paying for Productivity*. Ed. A. Blinder. Washington, D.C.: Brookings Institution.

Dornbusch, Rudiger, and Sebastian Edwards. 1990. "The Economic Populism Paradigen." NBER Working Paper, May.

Dyba, Karel, and Martin Kupka. 1990. "Economic Relations with Market Economies: The Case of Czechoslovakia." Working Paper, Prague.

Grosfeld, Irena. 1990. "Privatization of State Enterprises in Eastern Europe: The Search for Environment." Delta, Doc. No. 90-17, Paris.

Hanusch, Horst, ed. 1988. *Evolutionary Economics*. Cambridge: Cambridge University Press.

Lubos, Mlcoch. 1989. "Behavior of Czechoslovak Enterprises." Research Paper No. 348. Prague: Institute of Economics.

McDermott, Gerald, and Michal Mejstrik. 1990. "Czechoslovak Competitiveness and the Role of Small Firms." Paper for WZB Conference, Berlin.

Mejstrik, Michal. 1990. "Innovation and Technology Transfer." Conference Proceedings. Prague: Institute of Economics.

Mizsei, Kalman. 1990. "Experiences with Privatization in Hungary." World Bank Conference, Washington, D.C.

Svejnar, Jan. 1989. "A Framework for the Economic Transformation of Czechoslovakia." *PlanEcon Report* 5, 52, New York.

6

German Reunification and the Problems of the Czechoslovak Economy

Oldrich Dedek

A reunited Germany will have profound impact on Czechoslovakia, with both positive and negative effects for the smaller country's economy. This paper will explore those effects as well as examine some of the policy options facing the Czech government.

CZECHOSLOVAKIA'S RELATIONSHIP WITH GERMANY

Germany was the most important trading partner of prewar Czechoslovakia, despite the fact that its share of total Czech exports and imports had been gradually decreasing, from 33 percent in 1925 to 16 percent in 1937. During that period, Czechoslovakia's trade balance with Germany showed a slight deficit, though Czechoslovakia's overall trade balance usually was in surplus.

In the postwar period one can see the renewed importance of trade with what then became West Germany and East Germany. East Germany's share of Czechoslovak foreign trade rose from 1 percent in 1948 to approximately 7–8 percent in 1989. West Germany's share, in turn, rose from 1.5 percent in 1948 to 8–9 percent in 1989. Trade with both German nations amounted to 15–17 percent of total Czechoslovak exports and imports, which means that the unified Germany is Czechoslovakia's second largest trade partner after the Soviet Union.

There are several reasons why Germany is such an important trade partner:

1. The geographical proximity between the two countries means low transportation costs.
2. The deep cultural and historical contacts between the two countries has resulted in similar consumption patterns and skills.
3. Trade between East Germany and Czechoslovakia was for years cemented by bilateral agreements between the two centrally planned economies. East Germany was considered a reliable trade partner and a supplier of the most progressive articles within the Council of Mutual Economic Assistance. The production structures of East Germany and Czechoslovakia are in many aspects complementary. West Germany, meanwhile, is the major source of new technology and high-quality products and is one of Czechoslovakia's most important creditors. Czechoslovakia, in turn, exports raw materials; agricultural, chemical, and other less-manufactured products; and some consumer goods to West Germany.

Czechoslovakia's high dependence on trade with Germany contrasts with the unimportance of the inverse relationship. It is evident if we match the current 15–17 percent share of total Czechoslovak exports and imports with both German territories with the fact that the same indicator viewed from the German side seems to exceed—due to domination of the East by the West only marginally—the current 0.5 percent accounted for Czechoslovakia in total western German trade. Any disturbance in trade between Czechoslovakia and the reunified Germany will thus have a much greater effect on the Czechoslovak economy and can therefore seriously aggravate its transition process.

NEGATIVE IMPACTS OF REUNIFICATION

Eastern Germany will no longer demand many Czech goods because it will be able to find higher-quality products in its new domestic market. The Czechoslovak consumer goods industry is expected to be hardest hit by German reunification because eastern German consumers will have the affluent supply from western Germany at their disposal.

Tourism will also be affected seriously. Increasingly, eastern Germans will take advantage of their hard currency to travel more to South Europe. At the same time, Czechoslovak citizens' lack of hard currency means that fewer will visit eastern Germany.

Western Germany's preoccupation with the reunification will focus on the formation of a united German market, which means trade relations with Czechoslovakia will decline in importance. Experts predict Czechoslovakia will face increasingly weak export opportunities in fuels, raw materials, and intermediate products. Traditional exports of machines and transportation equipment appear to be declining as well. If Czechoslovakia's past trade deficit with West Germany foreshadows its trade relations with the reunified Germany, there is a danger of long-term and permanent trade disequilibrium between the two countries.

POSITIVE IMPACTS OF REUNIFICATION

There are, of course, some beneficial trends that Czechoslovakia can count on. Consider the following:

1. The process of reunification is expected to become an impetus for economic growth in Germany. Firms in western Germany will be investing in eastern Germany. This economic growth is likely to mean increased demand for imports, which will benefit the small European countries.

2. After reunification, eastern German enterprises will find themselves in competitive markets, which will force them to restructure, modernize, and look for outlets for produced goods. The well-established economic contacts with Czechoslovakia surely will be utilized. On the other hand, the wages of Czech workers will be low in terms of the deutsche mark, which could benefit Czech goods exported to the German market from the point of view of price competition.

The injection of German funds into the eastern region—necessary to a modernization policy as well as job creation—will have a spillover effect in Czechoslovakia.

COSTS OF MONETARIST-TYPE REFORM

Czechoslovakia, like its eastern German neighbor, has freely opted for a market economy. The problem facing the new government is not whether or not to create a free market, but how to successfully create it. Czech economists have differing views on this issue. Liberal economists consider the government incapable of creating an efficient pattern of economic production. The possibility of creating a priori a sound economic structure is a myth, confirmed by the poor results of the planned economy experiment. According to this view, the only sensible course the government can engage in is to restore, as quickly as possible, a market in which prices are allowed to move freely and competition is encouraged.

Gradual price reform is criticized for creating strong inflationary pressures, discriminating against producers who remain under price control, and allowing an inefficient allocation of resources to continue. The government decided to opt for full price liberalization, a policy manifest in the proposal to free prices as of January 1, 1991. Tight monetary and fiscal policies are expected to prevent inflation from soaring.

The opponents of this liberal view argue that text-book propositions that show why free prices are beneficial should be accompanied by other propositions that highlight the negative effects of a market economy. For example, along with competitive markets, free markets can also produce monopolies and oligopolies, which, in turn, can hinder the efficient allocation of resources. At the same time, there is a high degree of monopoly power. The supply of many goods is commonly dominated by one decisive domestic producer. In the composition of industry there is a vacuum in small and medium-sized firms, as is demonstrated by the fact that the average number of workers per firm is about 4,000, compared to 300 to 500 workers in Western Europe.

It is clear that the small size of the Czech economy hinders the introduction of competition from within. Foreign competition is needed both in the form of imports of goods and of capital, but the impact of foreign competition may be stalled by protectionist policies. Policymakers hope to protect domestic industries because Czechoslovak producers' technical backwardness and lack of experience with open markets cannot be overcome in the short run.

Another criticism concerns the problem of market stability. This view focuses on how an economic system develops given its particular starting conditions and prevailing behavior patterns. In the Czechoslovak case, the concern is that the adjustment mechanism will not lead the economy smoothly and quickly toward equilibrium.

Critics of "radical reform" point out that Czechoslovakia's initial conditions are poor. In addition to deep shortages in many markets, such as raw material, energy, and hard currency, some important markets (the capital market, for example) are nonexistent or are just being born (the labor and exchange markets, for example). Producers in the dominant state sector are more interested in payroll than in reinvesting their earnings. These are the major forces that will shape the dynamic trajectory.

Many critics believe these forces, combined with the rapid introduction of a market system, will lead the economy straight to hell. Price liberalization will cause the prices of raw materials, energy, and intermediate products to skyrocket. The exchange rate will climb to approximately 30 crowns per dollar before items can be exported profitably. The domestic market will be empty, as reduced domestic supply fuels inflationary pressures and increases the amount of expensive imported inputs. The result will be a massive number of defaults.

If the government is successful in enforcing a tight monetary policy, one can expect unemployment to climb sharply. If the government gives in to pressure for wage increases, the wage-price spiral will move into motion. Overall, liberal economists are accused of offering the causal series: inflation — restriction — recession.

Critics of liberals argue that the installment of the market during deep and plentiful disequilibrium is a grave mistake. They also believe that the initial restructuring of the economy by the government should be the government's responsibility. A sharp, selective restriction of business investment and consumption is recommended to ensure a more balanced starting position before the prices are allowed to move freely. The key thesis is that the basic restrictive policies can be initiated under conditions of an underdeveloped market, that one can, without correct price signals, roughly recognize what is and is not advantageous. After the governmental regulative measures remove the most obvious shortages, the individual segments can be integrated into one interlocked market.

It is no surprise that there is deep debate over how this historical experiment with the transition from a centrally planned economy to a market-based one should be conducted. The liberals stress minimal government involvement in the spontaneous market game. They emphasize the self-regulatory power of a market in allocating scarce resources more efficiently and removing disequilibrium more quickly than any other kind of coordination.

The interventionists' philosophy focuses on various forms of market failures and argues that the real market is far from being perfect. The government must step in and correct the errors. The government surely cannot avoid failures of its own, but interventionists believe that the government is sufficiently intelligent to avoid allowing itself to become the source of systematic disturbances in the economy.

Which group of economists is correct? Let us return to the German example, which provides some clues.

EASTERN GERMANY'S TRANSITION
TO A WESTERN-STYLE ECONOMY

Eastern German reform is radical, with the infusion of western German capital encouraging the development of competition. Although western German firms are playing a dominant role in eastern Germany, eastern Germans do not have to fear their economy being "sold out" to foreigners. Their economic affairs are taken over again by Germans themselves.

This radical reform has high social costs. Without western German assistance, there would be extensive long-term unemployment and/or a low standard of living in eastern Germany. Many products will not be able to face competition. Industrial products, which make up 45 to 50 percent of employment, will be most affected. But even in the presence of massive western German assistance due to lower labor productivity, obsolete machines, and restructuring, unemployment estimates span from 1.2 to 3 million people (15 to 30 percent of the labor force). The estimates are more than two times normal unemployment levels in western Germany. The transition in eastern Germany is a measurable demonstration of how difficult it is to create an efficient market mechanism out of a planned economy beset by allocative and internal inefficiencies.

Eastern Germany will not oppose western Germany paying for reunification if it can soften the impact of some of these social costs. Western Germany will carry out extensive transfers to help narrow the gap in wages between eastern and western Germany in order to slow undesired migration within the country. Western Germany also will assist in paying out unemployment and retirement benefits. Finance assistance is expected to improve eastern Germany's neglected infrastructure.

To summarize, the German model of transition from a centrally planned economy to a market-based one contains unique, nontransferable features. To protect its own national identity, at the beginning of the reform process Czechoslovakia will be less open to foreign competition than eastern Germany. Czechoslovakia cannot count on the high level of financial aid eastern Germany will receive, which will enable eastern Germany to soften the impact of reform on living standards.

The only feature common for both eastern Germany and other Eastern European countries is that radical reform has high social costs. Policymakers should therefore strive to create a balance between the hardship of restructuring and various forms of compensations. The liberal prescriptions seem to neglect this balance, which is crucial to creating a viable reform project.

7

Germany:
The Locomotive of
Eastern European Privatization

Jenik Radon

The year 1989 was one of political euphoria in the West and, even more so, in Eastern Europe. One Communist regime after another surrendered its stranglehold on political power in Poland, Hungary, East Germany, and Czechoslovakia. Even Romania and Bulgaria could not maintain business as usual, as the communists in those countries had to rename and restructure themselves, even if violently, as in the case of Romania. Loss of one-party political power also ushered in the beginning of decentralized economic decisionmaking and awakened the dream of more prosperous times. Privatization of the Eastern European economies became a stated goal, especially in Hungary and Poland. However, the political changes in 1989 were so rapid that little thought could be given to a comprehensive, let alone clear, definition of that term or the process that it should take.

The year 1990 dawned with a cold shower for many of the people of Eastern Europe. It was a shower that could not be turned off. Poland ushered in a radical program of economic shock therapy in an effort to commercialize its economy and make it subject to free-market or capitalistic principles. In this regard, the program's immediate goal was to bring under control a devastating inflation of more than 800 percent per annum. It succeeded, but not without steadily growing unemployment. In addition, the program's authors wanted to effect a restructuring of the economy from one based on state or government ownership of property to one based on private ownership. In short, the program sought the privatization of the entire Polish economy. The process, however, has so far defied speedy implementation. In fact, the lack of speed has given the Polish national hero, Lech Walesa, a political battle cry.

Although government-owned industries and companies in England, New Zealand, and other nations had been, or are being, privatized, no nation had yet sought to privatize (or more accurately, reprivatize) an entire economy. Consequently, it was no surprise that the concept of privatization, and what its implementation entails, was not, and could not be, fully appreciated, especially with the emphasis on the radical and revolutionary moment. Privatization had become intellectually and emotionally synonymous with the transformation of a centrally planned economy into a market economy. The assumption and belief was that a market economy could not be achieved as long as there was substantial state ownership of property. But how one effected such a change of ownership appeared to defy explanation. In a comical, almost hopeless refrain, the issue was phrased: "How do you make fish out of fish soup?"

PRIVATIZATION AND WHAT IT MEANS

As a consensus appeared to evolve, privatization can now be said to be primarily aimed at significantly increasing capital investment, both domestic and foreign, creating a self-sustaining private sector with a significant middle class by establishing small and medium-sized firms, reducing substantially the size and influence of the state sector, and dismantling state monopolies. Still, the speed at which this process can or should take place is hotly debated, if not outrightly disputed. Czechoslovakia is locked in an intellectual battle pitting heartfelt socialists against capitalist or market-oriented reformers. The result is that Czechoslovakia, which has been renamed the Czech and Slovak Federative Republic in response to the political demands of the Slovak minority, has to date only firmly committed to restoring the ownership of small businesses and services to private control. The transfer of the ownership of large enterprises from the state to that of individuals and privately owned companies raises in the minds of the Eastern European reformers and populace ethical issues of fairness and equity. It is feared that such a transfer will clearly result in the enriching of some at the expense of society and all of its citizens. Thus, this legacy of socialism, namely a system of perceived equality for all, adversely affects the publicly stated commitment of the newly elected governments of the nations of Eastern Europe to the quick implementation of a privatization process.

Privatization has also been set back by the fear of a "sell-out." Hungary's love affair with foreign investment soured when Austrian investment bankers, together with their Hungarian partners, earned an undisclosed but apparently significant fee on the sale of a 50 percent interest in the crown jewel of the Hungarian economy, Tungsram, a light-bulb manufacturer, to an American company, General Electric. Hungarians, fearful that their country was being sold to foreigners at bargain-basement prices, immediately adopted laws that made the purchase of interests in Hungarian enterprises by foreign parties more cumbersome and difficult. The role or function of independent advisers and so-called middlemen, such as investment bankers, was also called into question by Hungarian politicians in response public concerns.

The Privatization of Privatization

If the process of privatization is to attain a self-sustaining momentum, then the entire process will have to be privatized and be independent of public and political pressures. This means that the process itself must be decentralized and that the state control of the process must be decreased significantly. In brief, each enterprise, as well as a division or part of an enterprise, must be legally empowered to organize and implement its own privatization. A central administration is too cumbersome, too bureaucratic, and often not sufficiently knowledgeable about the business of a particular enterprise, to implement a speedy and timely privatization program. Admittedly, special legislation concerning self-dealing and other corrupt practices will have to be enacted and enforced.

Intellectual Battleground

As the year 1990 came to a close, the process of privatization in
Eastern Europe became a battleground for intellectuals, politicians,
bureaucrats, and fearful workers.   Still, the deteriorating economies of Hungary, the Czech and Slovak Federative Republic, and
Poland will exert their own reform pressures to ensure that the
process is not stopped, even if it is not advanced with the utmost
speed.   Even in the former East Germany bureaucrats were incapable of instituting an effective privatization program with the result that hundreds, if not thousands, of "West" German business
leaders have to be enlisted into the ranks of the *Treuhand*, the privatizing agency, to carry the process forward.   Also, although the role
of foreign capital has been questioned, the need for very significant
amounts of foreign capital, as well as western management and
training in the methods of the market economy, is not seriously
questioned or doubted.   There simply is no alternative because the
Eastern European countries themselves cannot generate the necessary funds.

THE GERMAN ECONOMY AND ITS *MITTELSTAND*

Germany, because of its geographical proximity to and extensive
trade with Eastern Europe, its vibrant economy, and a host of other
factors, including its ongoing, day-to-day experience in privatizing
the economy of the former East Germany, can, and will, serve as
the locomotive of the Eastern European privatization process.
German importers and exporters, as well as investors, by their very
nature will, directly and indirectly, encourage the establishment
in Eastern Europe of many small and mid-sized firms.   In fact, the
structure of the Germany economy, which for the purposes of this
paper means the former West Germany unless otherwise indicated, will also serve as a model for the restructuring of Eastern
Europe.

The strength of the German economy is based on its relatively
unique structure.   It is not an economy with a significant number of
large companies.   Only about 3 percent of the world's largest 1,000
corporations are German firms.   The United States and Japan, with

populations that are, respectively, four and two times larger than Germany, each have more than ten times as many companies in the largest 1,000. The German economy is based on the so-called mid-sized firms, in German, the *mittelstand*. It is an express goal of the German government to recreate a *mittelstand* in the former East Germany so that the *mittelstand* can become the backbone of that region.

Although the United States also has many small and mid-sized firms, the *mittelstand* is the heart, as well as the dominating factor, of the German economy. It is responsible for making Germany the largest exporter in the world, and it accounts for approximately 80 percent of its GNP. In the German chemical industry, for example, which is a large-firm business in most nations, the *mittelstand* firms account for 75 percent of the industry's output. They also predominate in the machine tool trade, which, together with the automobile industry, ranks as Germany's premier export; indeed, Germany claims about 24 percent of the world machine tool market.

Sales of *mittelstand* firms range widely, from a few million deutsche mark to a few hundred million deutsche mark, and such firms are often privately held. Many are family-owned companies and are financially supported by their "house bank," namely, the bank with which they have had a long-standing, almost exclusive, relationship. But they also share a number of characteristics, described in greater detail below.

A *Mittelstand* Firm

The Vetter pharmaceutical company in Ravensburg, Germany, is typical of a successful *mittelstand* firm. It is a world-class manufacturer of a limited number of specialized pharmaceutical products, in particular, patented dual-chamber syringes. A significant portion of its sales is exported, and exports are a steadily growing aspect of its business. Its management, technically trained and educated, is small in number and has a hands-on, flexible approach. The company's strengths are in supporting continuous innovative improvements in its product-line as well as in the manufacturing process and in encouraging a team-work approach in dealing with its customers. Although such characteristics are not uncommon for an internationally recognized pharmaceutical company, Vetter is a family-owned company with 450 employees, all well trained and quality conscious, successfully competing in its niche market with global giants. Further, the high standards of the pharmaceutical industry, necessitated by the obvious dictates of medical work, as exemplified by Vetter, are also characteristic of the machine tool and many other German *mittelstand* industries.

Vetter does not have any manufacturing facilities outside of Germany, but Vetter has a substantial export trade and imports many of its supplies. Although Vetter does not source its supplies from Eastern Europe, a large and growing number of *mittelstand* firms do. However, an increasing number of German companies have found that many state-owned enterprises, as well as newly established private firms, including cooperatives, in Eastern Europe are unable to deliver quality products in a timely manner. This has prompted many to establish Eastern European joint ventures in order to gain control over quality, production, scheduling, and other elements of the manufacturing process. Of course, Germans also have other motivations for the establishment of joint ventures, including lower production costs and ground-floor entrance to a potentially expanding market.

Joint Ventures and Export

Eastern European joint-venture undertakings by the German *mittelstand* are not simply company expansion for its own sake or the pursuit of a version of the popular American corporate game, mergers and acquisitions. For the *mittelstand* firm, such investment is often conceived as a way of strengthening domestic (that is, German) production and more firmly securing a particular export market for German products. With such a global approach, Germany has secured its position as the world's largest trading country and as the number one trading partner for Eastern Europe and the Soviet Union. Its exports, with their reputation for quality and reliability, are the most sought-after western commodities in those nations. This does not even take into account the trading relations of the former East Germany.

German corporations generally prefer to engage in standard straight-forward buy and sell (or import-export) transactions and not establish a joint venture with a foreign partner. The organization of any partnership has its problems, especially if different cultures and customs, and in turn business philosophies, must be welded into one. Still, the *mittelstand* firms do enter into joint ventures in Eastern Europe. In Poland, Hungary, and the Soviet Union, German companies have established the plurality of all joint ventures and constitute, for example, about 40 percent of all Polish joint ventures. *Mittelstand* business leaders, representing thousands of firms, are actively looking for purchasers of their exports and are willing, if not always eager, to enter into joint ventures, including manufacturing joint ventures, to ensure their export success.

It is not unusual for a German machine tool company, for example, to establish a joint venture that produces the necessary spare parts for one or more of the company's products. The availability of spare parts in the local foreign market will normally fuel a demand for the more sophisticated machine tool, namely the higher value-added product produced by the German parent company. If such demand does not materialize or proves insufficient, the spare parts can usually be exported to support the German company's overall international export activity.

The *Mittelstand* and its Eastern European Joint Venture Counterpart

The preferable joint venture partners of a *mittelstand* firm are companies of comparable or smaller size. And, surprisingly for acquisition-minded American firms, many joint ventures with *mittelstand* partners have not come from hastily negotiated and arranged courtships but have evolved naturally out of pre-existing business relationships with the Eastern European importers of the *mittelstand's* firms' products. In the past, such Eastern European companies have been cooperatives and divisions of state-owned enterprises, a distinctive part that could be separately incorporated into a self-sustaining company. The resultant joint ventures are often smaller firms with a relatively small capitalization. Both by seeking smaller partners and organizing small or mid-sized joint ventures, the *mittelstand* firms are indirectly encouraging the formation of their mirror image, namely Eastern European small and mid-sized companies, and therefore also the creation of an entrepreneurial middle class. Thousands of *mittelstand* firms are thus furthering the primary goals of Eastern European privatization.

The *mittelstand's* technically experienced hands-on management can more easily and flexibly interact with the responsible managers of many Eastern European firms, many of whom are also technically educated. Further, such technical background on the part of the Eastern Europeans permits them to more easily comprehend the complexities of building a modern manufacturing facility, as well as appreciate the need for quality control, even if they have not in the past been able or sufficiently concerned, whether because of a lack of incentive or motivation or a shortage of funds or sophisticated demand, to introduce internationally recognized quality-control procedures and standards. In furthering business ties, the Germans invariably require their Eastern European management and their staffs to receive on-the-job training, frequently in Germany. Further, because the *mittelstand* firm management is not heavily layered, an Eastern European has an opportunity to become an integral part of the management team. German businesses have in the past accepted many Eastern Europeans into their ranks, especially those with scientific or technical backgrounds who speak German and have learned the German way of doing things. This type of flexibility is otherwise only evident in American firms.

Mittelstand Firm: The Transferor of Western Business Practices

It has been reported that about 12,000 Soviets will participate in primarily industry-sponsored on-the-job training programs of varying durations during the next few years throughout Germany. Even if such persons should leave the employ of a Soviet trading partner of a German company or a German-Soviet joint venture, these people will invariably think of the German products manufactured by the firms in which they trained. Their exposure to Germany will invariably increase the demand for German products and therefore German exports. Thus, at the minimum, the training of Eastern Europeans is the best, and perhaps least expensive, form of advertising for German companies.

There are thousands of business leaders from *mittelstand* firms eagerly looking for niche positions in Eastern Europe, many of whom are, or report directly to, the decisionmakers of their firms and are not just representatives of the world's Fortune 1,000. In the first instance, the resultant business will consist of trade. And thereafter applying the on-ground information gained through ongoing trading activities, these business leaders will seek investment opportunities. Thus, the German *mittelstand* will transmit its needs and demands for working with smaller, high-quality-oriented firms to its Eastern European counterparts. This will be made easier for these German firms, as their many representatives will necessarily come into contact with a very broad spectrum of the Eastern European population, in particular its emerging entrepreneurial middle class.

Moreover, the German *mittelstand* firm, because it is relatively small, will establish a close, almost intimate relationship with its Eastern European joint venture and investment and trading partners. The Eastern European firm will also come to envision its own future because it hopes that it will become a mirror reflection of its partner, the German *mittelstand* firm. In turn, the Germans will become the main transferor of western market-oriented business principles to Eastern Europe and maintain their position as the leading foreign economic participants in Eastern Europe.

THE LESSON FOR THE UNITED STATES

Americans and other economic competitors of the Germans will only be able to successfully compete in Eastern Europe if export consciousness becomes broadly based among American firms and is not just limited to the Fortune 1,000. Further, on-the-job training by U.S. companies for thousands of Eastern Europeans, and not just for MBA graduates, must become the norm. The United States should make the issuances of short-term training visas automatic to any American corporation willing to sponsor an Eastern European. The challenge of German competition should also encourage the

Department of Commerce and the Small Business Administration to support a combined program of export promotion and on-the-job training in the United States, especially in the many smaller and mid-sized U.S. companies. Until an army of American business leaders combs the Eastern European marketplace and allows trading relationships to evolve naturally into business partnerships, the United States will miss many opportunities for investment, not to mention exports. Further, the United States will have denied itself the opportunity to have a broad impact on the privatization of Eastern Europe and to become *a*, if not *the*, locomotive of change there.

8

Investment Opportunities in a Unified Germany

David B. Audretsch and Heather L. Wayland

According to Norbert Walter, chief economist of the Deutsche Bank, the economic and monetary union of July 1, 1990, will inject new life into an already booming West German economy. Production in West Germany will go up by more than 3.5 percent this year, and "an 8 percent growth rate for East Germany in the next five years is thoroughly realistic."[1] Indeed, while business upswings historically tend to level out after about three years, West Germany has been growing steadily since 1982, and Walter's projections would suggest that this unusual trend may continue well into 1995 and beyond. Thus, GNP in the unified Germany is estimated to approach DM27 billion, with less than DM22 emanating from what is called, since unification, "western Germany." In the midst of such optimism, however, an unexpected number of potential investors in "eastern Germany" are still holding back. This analysis is an attempt to explain why. The radical economic and political reforms of German unification have brought (and will continue to bring) a host of new dangers—as well as opportunities—and neither the difficulties of surviving the transition to a market economy nor the uncertainties and costs of this historic experiment should be underestimated. In this paper we will depict the dilemma now confronting the eastern German economy,

---

1. "Interview: Norbert Walter zur deutschen Konjunktur." *Wirtschaftswoche*, June 22, 1990, p. 29.

highlight the underlying structural causes, and analyze the risks and opportunities of investing in this newly opened market.

ECONOMIC AND MONETARY UNION

On July 1, 1990, the West German mark was officially introduced into East Germany, replacing the Ostmark and thereby opening the economy to the competitive realities of the world market. On the same day, East Germany abandoned its forty-year framework of imposing regulations and adopted West German welfare, insurance, corporate, and union legislation. The implications of these reforms were enormous. Most importantly, economic and monetary union implied the restoration of property rights; homes were not only freed for long-needed repairs but could also be used as collateral for loans to start new businesses. And by removing legal restrictions on the sale of land, the process of privatizing industry could finally begin to accelerate. A second key implication was the liberalization of trade. With the elimination of former subsidies and the deregulation of almost all prices, officials hoped to bring greater structural transparency into the economic sphere.

On December 2, 1990, an all-national vote made the unification process complete. Full economic, social, and political integration, however, will take years and presents great risks and opportunities for western investors. As long as the massive unemployment and social unrest brought about by such a shock therapy can be kept within boundaries, eastern Germany's transformation will be far less traumatic than that of its Eastern European neighbors. Eastern Germany has been given the unique opportunity to begin its future with a hard currency, a vital prerequisite for attracting western investors and increasing interaction between the western and eastern German economies. While Poland and Hungary will be forced to create their own convertible currency, the deutsche mark has guaranteed eastern Germany free entrance to international capital markets.

Despite this head start, the introduction of western currency is only the first step on the long and rocky road toward recovery. West German Chancellor Helmut Kohl can expect to fight hard to maintain his popularity in the months ahead. Indeed, the Christian Democrats' "cold turkey" tactics for a speedy unification have triggered an ominous wave of unemployment, and although Bonn is already selling over US$70 million in bonds to add to the social safety net, even this may not be enough. By early July, about 223,000 of eastern Germany's 8.5 million workers had already lost their jobs, and another 500,000 had been placed on shortened shifts under a special DM2 billion (US$1.22 billion) compensation plan.

According to Peter Danylow, a German analyst for the Foundation for Sciences and Policy outside Munich, "Certain East German industry sectors are in deep need of help because they simply can't produce efficiently, particularly agricultural and consumer goods. And if the trend continues, we could well see an outburst of social unrest and another mass migration to the west." Unfortunately, this nightmare may already be coming true. According to official estimates, unemployment rolls are swelling at a rate of between 30,000 to 40,000 every week, and Labor and Social Affairs Minister Regine Hildebrandt is anticipating unemployment to rise soon from 220,000 to 1.5 million.

THE CAUSES UNDERLYING THE CRISIS

While monetary and currency union has clearly triggered eastern Germany's current wave of bankruptcies and unemployment, three major structural deficiencies are the root causes of the country's problems: the misallocation of resources, low levels of worker motivation, and the lethargic inflexibility of the over-sized combines.

Throughout the 1980s the international competitiveness of East German goods decreased steadily, and the foreign worth of the currency dropped by 50 percent. This is largely attributable to the corporate-like structures called combines, which were giant firms formed during the previous three decades by lumping together, on average, twenty to forty plants. As each combine strove to become its own closed economic sphere, the flexibility of the individual plant was sharply diminished. The process of centralization under the system of combines had a dramatic impact on the structure of manufacturing industries in East Germany. Table 8-1 shows the drastic decrease in the number of manufacturing plants (betriebe), from 11,253 in 1971 to 3,449 in 1987.[2] Particularly striking is the virtual eradication of smaller-sized plants over this period. The East German policy of centralization and the de facto elimination of smaller plants and firms under the *kombinate* system provide a striking contrast to the entrepreneurial revolution and explosion in the number of new small firms and plants in western economies, particularly the United States. The absence of such entrepreneurial activity deprived East Germany of the engine of innovation and the greatest source of dynamism in the West.

With the state determining the allocation of resources, investment was concentrated in certain industries (such as microelectronics) in a desperate attempt to raise East Germany's productivity to world standards. These industries generally benefited from preferred treatment, but the government's policy had two shortcomings: production levels continued to remain disappointingly low,[3] and investment and innovation in other areas (especially consumer goods) were neglected. A final problem was the workforce itself. Over 8 million (of a total workforce of 8.5 million) were employed by socialist firms, mainly the several hundred combines. After years of watching their profits being funneled directly to the government, workers contented themselves with their lifetime contracts. Not surprisingly, motivation lagged. Excessive attention in meeting purely quantitative production goals, rather than maximizing quality and minimizing production costs, also reinforced a lack of innovation.

Overall, productivity in East Germany was less than 50 percent below that of West Germany. For those concerned about keeping up with international competition, this was a sobering figure. Immediate disaster could be averted by minimizing domestic consumption and utilizing export capacities to their limits, but this approach would only disguise the severity of the problem. The costs of neglected investment became increasingly manifest, import needs steadily increased, and the foreign debt grew to around US$20 billion.

2. Including nonmanufacturing as well as manufacturing, establishments totaled 8,000 in 1987.
3. Despite favored state funding, East Germany's microelectronics industry remained six to eight years behind that of West Germany.

Table 8-1. Number of Plants in Eastern German Manufacturing by Size 1971–1987

Number of Workers and Employees	1971	1978	1987
Less than 25	3864	716	131
26–50	2559	1084	186
51–100	1812	1130	343
101–200	1147	946	519
201–500	845	1074	861
501–1000	405	517	558
1001–2500	406	480	540
2501–5000	133	178	215
5001–10000	62	69	75
10001–20000	15	16	21
20000 +	5	3	—
Total	11253	6213	3449

Source: *Statistisches Jahrbuch der DDR*, various years. Adapted from Hans-Gerd Bannasch, "The Evolution of Small Business in East Germany," in Z. Acs and D. B. Audretsch, eds., *Entrepreneurship in East and West Countries, A Global Perspective* (Cambridge: Cambridge University Press), 1991.

CONTEMPORARY RESTRUCTURING MEASURES
IN EASTERN GERMANY

Even after economic and monetary union, eastern Germany's international competitiveness is still unclear.   Yet by exposing an
economy whose level of development remains twenty to twenty-five
years behind that of western Germany to a shock of this kind, an
irreversible and risky experiment has begun.   Lacking quality, an
image, and competitive prices, eastern German industry has been
hit hard by an invasion of western goods.   According to eastern
German reports, at least 30 percent of eastern Germany's 8,000
state-owned *volkseigenebetriebe* (VEBs) are completely insolvent and
unable to pay wages or purchase materials.[4]   For western Germany's *Treuhandanstalt*, the state trust agency responsible for
privatization and the organization of state-owned combines and
smaller businesses, the task of aiding struggling firms, dissolving
cartels, and finding interested buyers has proven to be formidable.
The agency is armed with DM17 billion in restructuring credits to
be given out by the end of 1991, but the liquidation credits for wages
and materials are still far from sufficient. Lacking time for managerial, product, and workforce readjustment, eastern German industry is also burdened by a cumulative debt of DM100 billion.
Critics claim that potentially competitive firms are being allowed
to die out.

Part of the problem, of course, is the lack of interested investors.
Of the 8,000 VEBs currently in the government's trusteeship
(estimated to be worth DM600 billion), officials expect to sell only
DM1 billion worth of holdings this year.   While Burger King,
Siemens, Lufthansa, Daimler Benz, GM, and Volkswagen are
among the handful of pioneers entering joint ventures with state
enterprise spin-offs, the demand for capital continues to exceed the
supply.   Given the continuing legal and economic uncertainties, as
well as eastern Germany's inherited history of low productivity,
burdensome debts, and even more cumbersome red tape, the hesi-
tancy of most private investors remains high—thus leaving the
enormous task of restructuring to the state.   While isolated success

---

4. A *volkseigenebetrieb*, a plant owned by the government, usually belongs to a combine.

stories helped to reinstall the trust agency's hope for the privatization process, most eastern German industries are floundering.[5] By July 1, 1990, over 40 percent of all larger firms had applied for financial help, totaling more than DM5 million. Whether these calls for help can be answered, and whether this money will indeed be effective in reviving the ailing enterprises, remains unclear.

For the 12,000 medium-sized firms nationalized in 1972, the picture is at least somewhat brighter.[6] The *Treuhandanstalt* approved 582 joint ventures for small and medium-sized firms, compared to only seventeen joint ventures with former combines and VEBs. Meanwhile, a number of former owners have applied to the state for repossession. They have offered to repay the firms' price at nationalization and are haggling over the value of subsequent state investments. Hopes are high that with modern technology and equipment, productivity can quickly return to West German standards. The European Recovery Program has already handed out US$3.5 billion in loans to support would-be entrepreneurs, and it is assumed that this sector of medium-sized firms will be privatized quickly.

Despite the crippling effects of union demands, profit-restricting legal requirements, and massive and widespread uncertainty, progress has been made in reprivatizing combines, VEBs, and the *mittelstand*, while an increasing number of new reforms are being established. By the end of May 1990, there were 59,435 registered new start-ups, 60 percent in the service sector and tourism. According to Norbert Walter and other economists, the long-neglected service sector will soon experience a healthy boom, spurring growth in other sectors as well. According to others, however, such optimism is unfounded. The current number of joint ventures remains significantly below expectations, and unless investors become less hesitant, eastern Germany is destined for hard times ahead.

5. For example, VEB Polygraph. Polygraph's five principal industries, all of which make sophisticated printing equipment and are international leaders in their fields, provide natural and attractive units for division and resale.

6. Large plants and firms were nationalized shortly after East Germany was created in 1949.

SOME GOOD REASONS NOT TO INVEST
IN EASTERN GERMANY

1. *Low Productivity.* Product quality aside, eastern German produc-
    tivity averages half that of western Germany, and in some sec-
    tors sinks to 25 percent or even lower. There are a variety of
    reasons contributing to the gap:

    a. outdated technology and worn-out equipment;
    b. poor management;
    c. inefficient organization and allocation of resources;
    d. unreliable suppliers;
    e. an extremely neglected infrastructure, especially in the
        transportation and communication sectors;
    f. lack of motivation among the workforce;
    g. lack of highly qualified workers; and
    h. lag in research and development, combined with a
        failure to apply new knowledge to production.

    Without even attempting to weight these factors, it quickly
    becomes apparent that eastern Germany's structurally embed-
    ded deficiencies ripple throughout the entire economy. And it
    is precisely because these deficiencies are structural that their
    elimination or reduction will prove so difficult.

    Most importantly, it will take time. According to numerous
    reports in the business press, most factories are in fact not
    worth modernizing and must be rebuilt from scratch. The pro-
    cess of taking over modern product licenses, replacing old
    hardware, and retraining workers could take several years.
    While short-run productivity can be increased with better
    management and more reliable material delivery, reformers
    (especially in the industrial sector) are swimming upstream,
    and catching up with the west will not be easy.

2. *Impending High Wages.* At first glance, eastern German wages
    seem nothing less than an investor's dream. Averaging
    US$5.40 per hour (less than one-third of western German
    levels in some industries), they are well below western
    German wages. This gap might appear to more than compen-
    sate for eastern Germany's low productivity. However, an in-

vestor's optimism may be dampened by the following dilemma: Eastern German wages should rise in order to prevent extensive emigration to the west, but they must also remain sufficiently low in order to attract investors. These conflicting goals have caused substantial unrest among workers and investors alike. Because productivity and product quality is low, many industrial branches can only be competitive through correspondingly low prices. Unfortunately, this can only be achieved through wages so minimal that westward emigration is accelerated. Multitudes of educated eastern German workers have already exercised their newly won mobility and left for more lucrative jobs in the west.

The situation is precarious, and so far eastern Germany's trade unions have not made things any easier. Clinging like true socialists to strict egalitarian norms, union activists are opposing wage differential according to qualification or skill and demanding both shorter work weeks and higher wages.

If we take into account the effective loss of income that accompanied monetary union, the demand for higher wages is somewhat understandable. Eastern Germany's extremely low wages were only possible thanks to massive subsidization of consumer goods and a strong purchasing power not fully accounted for by official exchange rates. Taking into account purchasing power parities, one group of economists concluded that East German income levels before the 1989 revolution were significantly higher than those of Portugal, Greece, Ireland, and even Spain. With the elimination of subsidies and the flood of western goods, the costs of basic goods have skyrocketed, justifying (if not necessitating) higher wages.

This past dependence on reasonable living conditions, together with eastern Germany's psychological starting point—the presumption that unification can deliver wealth fast—is obviously fraught with dangers. In the short run these expectations can be somewhat controlled through transitional business subsidies and social security measures for the underpaid and laid-off workers. Such a policy in turn requires substantial financial cooperation from Bonn. If trade unions continue short-sighted attempts to attain too many benefits too fast, necessary investments may not materialize. Western German investments in the east that have a central role in reviving the eastern German economy are already below original expectations.[7] For eastern Germany to increase efforts to make its economy more attractive to potential investors it must restrict demands for higher wages and shorter workweeks and allow employers greater flexibility in determining a differentiated pay-scale according to individual skills, qualification, and overall productivity.

3. *Poor Infrastructure.* For forty years East German industry focused narrowly on increasing short-run productivity, neglecting almost completely the maintenance of its infrastructure. Today, this poses ominous obstacles to increasing efficiency, decreasing costs, and raising productivity. Consider some of the following deficiencies:

a. According to the German Institute for Economic Research, 60 percent of all city streets and 45 percent of all highways can be classified into the highest damage category. Repairs are an estimated DM100 billion.

b. Eastern German railways are run-down and unreliable. In addition to modernization, the network must be connected to the west—an undertaking requiring at least DM100 billion.

c. Eastern Germany has only one international airport (in East Berlin), which has a capacity of only 1.5 million passengers per year.

d. Only 16 percent of all households have phones, compared to 93 percent in western Germany. Even existing connections are poor and highly unreliable, especially between east and west. Over the next seven years, 8 million telephone connections are estimated to be installed as part of a DM55 billion job of bringing the eastern German system up to par.

e. Eastern German energy costs are 30 to 50 percent higher than those in western Germany. To protect struggling industries from a burden of this magnitude,

---

7. Western Germany is currently engaged in 96 percent of all joint ventures in eastern Germany.

the government has agreed to continue the subsidization of energy prices for industry, keeping them 30 percent below those of western Germany until 1993.
Western Germany, meanwhile, has the highest energy prices in all of Europe. This massive reconstruction will take at least a decade.

4. *Government Bureaucracy and Business Legislation.* Thanks to four
long decades of Communist rule and a correspondingly stub-
born bureaucracy, prospects for less restrictive business legislation and a quick resolution of property disputes in eastern
Germany appear bleak. The decision made in spring 1990 to
return or compensate for wrongfully dispossessed eastern
German homes and businesses to their original owners, predominantly in western Germany, has resulted in legal chaos.
Potential investors are likely to remain hesitant until the tens
of thousands of cases can be settled. Of course, the situation is
improving somewhat. In an April 1990 poll among eastern
German managers, 50 percent viewed government bureaucracy
and 56 percent saw business legislation as primary business obstacles. By May 1990, these figures had been reduced to 35 percent and 42 percent, respectively, with the focus shifting instead
toward a fundamental lack of capital. Western entrepreneurs,
however, continue to complain about endless red tape and an
anti-business attitude. Local officials, for example, have often
rejected proposals to set up new shops because there is "no
need" for the goods or services they plan to offer.

5. *Potential for Political Turmoil.* According to a June 1990 poll, approximately 80 percent of the eastern German population estimated the country's economic situation as poor. Yet while the
majority were able to recognize the current crisis on a theoret-
ical level, well over one-half estimated their personal situation
as "good." Such widespread, unfounded optimism cannot continue indefinitely. The length of the transition period is unknown, and as unemployment and wage dissatisfaction grows,
so too will the potential for disillusionment and social unrest.
On a large enough scale such widespread public dissatisfaction
could trigger a severe counter-revolution, while challenging
western Germany's commitment to a decentralized market
economy.

WHY INVESTING IN EASTERN GERMANY MAKES SENSE

1. *Potential for Rapid Productivity Growth.* According to the German Institute for Economic Research, overall productivity will double in the next ten years, reaching 80 percent of western German productivity by the year 2000.

   In many respects, the starting point of the eastern German economy is promising. In 1983, eastern Germany ranked fifteenth in GNP among industrial countries. Moreover, eastern Germany's education levels are high relative to European standards. While the proportion of college graduates is somewhat lower than that of western Germany, the percent of vocational-school graduates and certified apprentices is significantly higher.

2. *Short-run Wage Differentials.* Eastern German wages are already being pushed higher by the removal of subsidies and by increases in consumer goods prices. Nevertheless, current wage differentials between east and west are still substantial. Average wages remain a low DM1,700 per month (raised from DM1,292), and are still a significant 50 percent below western German levels (averaging DM4,035 in 1988). The service sector, where low wages are quickly accompanied by relatively high productivity, has a particularly promising outlook. As long as it remains possible to contain social unrest, emigration, and union demands, productivity growth stands to exceed wages and a significant number of businesses may prosper.

3. *Potential Quality of Future Infrastructure.* Despite today's unreliable network of phone lines and pothole-ridden streets, optimists insist on treating this vice as virtue. The radical restructuring of eastern Germany's infrastructure, they argue, has given the region the unique opportunity to utilize new technology and the potential to excel even internationally famed standards of western Germany. Using lessons from the west's postwar development, new technology (such as fiber optics and mobile communications) can be introduced from the start. While the source of the necessary DM30 billion per year is not yet clear, this capital investment program should boost the eastern German economy and prompt the creation of numerous service companies as well as additional joint ventures. While

few private investors have demonstrated a willingness to tackle eastern Germany's infrastructural dilemma, fearless capitalists have been found. For example, the chief of VUVG Telekom, Helmut Ricke, expects to spend more than US$34 billion in eastern Germany over the next decade and promises that by the end of the 1990s eastern Germany will have one of the world's most up-to-date phone systems.

4. *Years of Pent-Up Demand.* Although most eastern German households are quantitatively well equipped (99 percent of all households own a washing machine and 96 percent a television), product quality is low. Whereas consumers in the formerly noncompetitive market were willing to wait up to seventeen years and pay huge sums for such "luxury goods" as the infamous Trabi (the pet name of the East German automobile, Trabant), now these items are practically unsalable. Awed by the price, variety, and quality of western consumer goods, unprecedented numbers of easterners are swarming westward to exchange their cheaply made appliances for a more attractive selection of products. Western producers, meanwhile, are hoping to supply this growing demand by shipping mass quantities of their goods eastward.

5. *Leverage of Those with Capital.* Eastern Germany's dire need for outside investments is steadily increasing the leverage of those with capital. With no lack of criticism for union demands, business and government officials alike are aware of the necessity of creating a maximally favorable environment for investors. For the next two years any foreign investor can get a generous tax refund of 12 percent. Eastern German small and middle-sized firms are receiving a similar head start with rent subsidies of 50 percent. Nonetheless, even these incentives are not sufficient.

6. *Gateway to Eastern Europe.* Roughly two-thirds of eastern Germany's foreign trade is done with Eastern Bloc countries, primarily the Soviet Union. While relations with Poland, Hungary, and Czechoslovakia may decrease in relative importance as eastern Germany begins to look westward, the significance of these relations will ultimately increase. Thanks to the reunification process, eastern Germany seems to offer a more stable political environment than elsewhere in Eastern Europe

and is by far the most likely to survive the transition to a market economy. For eastern German economist Holle Grünert and many others, the future European economy promises to shift its center eastward. In this scenario, eastern Germany's cultural, historical, political, and economic ties to both east and west will become increasingly important.

7. *Foothold in the European Community.* Although foreign trade with European Community (EC) nations is currently only about 5 percent of eastern Germany's total foreign trade, this low figure will not last long. German reunification means that the eastern region will automatically share in membership in the EC. Western Germany's decision that all investment aid offered to Germans is available to all other EC members will introduce new trade patterns between east and west, as well as a wealth of new investment opportunities. The completion of the EC common market is expected to bring additional growth to Germany and reinforce an already booming economy.

CONCLUSION

The profitability of investing in eastern Germany is fundamentally dependent on the relationship between wages and productivity. Indeed, while prospects for rapid productivity appear hopeful, wage rate increases are also expected. As long as the productivity gains exceed the increase in the wage rates, foreign investment in eastern Germany will be attractive. To the extent that increased wages offset those productivity gains, however, the special advantages facing investors will be diminished. Those factors influencing either future productivity (such as infrastructure, skills and discipline of the labor force, and the rate of adaptation to technological change) or labor compensation (such as the adaptation of western German union, wage, and entitlement policies) will ultimately determine the extent to which foreign investment in the eastern part of a reunified Germany is worthwhile.

For a successful integration of eastern Germany in the west, three crucial policies must be implemented. First, the crippling legislation of the centralized government must be replaced by massive deregulation. In particular, the political and administrative barriers impeding the creation of new firms must be thoroughly and rapidly dismantled. Second, the economic assets currently held by the combines must be broken up into smaller units and shifted into private ownership. Such a process of privatization will facilitate the creation of an economic environment more conducive to urgently needed entrepreneurial activity. Finally, economic transactions based on free competition must replace the forty-year-old tradition of planning and cooperation. Replacing public monopolies with private ones, however, is certainly not the answer. The first days following currency and monetary union saw a handful of mergers involving large western German corporations taking over under-financed eastern German combines. The largest western German insurance company, Allianz, for example, is now (thanks to the successful completion of a hotly contested merger) a virtual monopolist in eastern Germany. While many in the eastern region rejoice at the entry of such large and established western German firms, the effective continuation of an oligopolistic market—whether dominated by the state or by western German companies—is hardly in the eastern German consumers' best interests. The high standard of living in western economies is attributable to the existence of highly competitive market economies, and in today's haste to attract western capital, this fact is all too easily forgotten. Investors will hopefully become less cautious, with encouragement coming from liberalized state legislation. Sobriety and caution are demanded from all sides. Eastern Germany is in dire need of an economic miracle, and this will require cooperation, time, capital, and good fortune.

9

Privatization Controversies
in the East and West

David P. Ellerman, Ales Vahcic, and Tea Petrin

"OWNERSHIP BY EVERYONE AND THUS BY NO ONE" IN THE EAST AND WEST

A large number of enterprises in communist and post-communist countries are "socially owned" instead of being state owned. The socially owned enterprises are formally controlled not by state ministries but by worker councils (Yugoslavia), enterprise councils (Hungary), or self-management councils (Poland). The de facto control group in the socially owned companies typically consists of managers, worker representatives, bankers, and local municipal authorities.

The control group in a socially owned enterprise does not have a recoupable claim on earnings reinvested in the firm. Retained profits become social property, property "owned by everyone and thus by no one." Hence, there is pressure to pay out the profits in an individualized form (for example, as bonuses) or to reinvest profits in a social way that will offset private expenditures (for example, company perquisites for managers and workers such as sports facilities, health clinics, and housing).

In their seminal work *The Modern Corporation and Private Property* (1932), Adolf Berle and Gardiner Means called attention to the "separation of ownership and control" in American corporations with widely dispersed and publicly traded equity shares. These companies are often called "public corporations," which should not be confused with government-owned corporations. Because equity

117

ownership in a public corporation is dissipated over a broad and ill-defined group of shareholders, the top managers together with their board of directors have "power without property."

Managers (and directors) typically have relatively small holdings of shares so the value that accrues to them from retained profits is small and distant compared to the value they can directly appropriate in salaries, bonuses, fees, and corporate perquisites. Hence, there is pressure for managers to expend corporate wealth in individually appropriable forms (compensation and perquisites), a tendency amply evidenced by comparing the salaries and benefits of executives in American public corporations with the significantly lower compensation of their counterparts in large Japanese corporations.

There are remarkable similarities between the state and socially owned firms of socialism and the public corporations of capitalism. Even the emerging managerialist ideology for the public corporations (paraphrased below) is strikingly "social-ist" without evoking any recognizable Marxist-socialist buzzwords.

> Managers have stewardship over the corporate resources in the interests of all the "stakeholders," not just the traditional shareholders. Any attempt to hold managers accountable to one particular private interest such as the stockholders would be to neglect the interests of the other stakeholders (employees, suppliers, consumers, and local residents). Managers must professionally balance the interests of the various stakeholders without capitulating to any specific private interest group.

And so forth. This idea that those in power cannot be held effectively accountable to any particular identifiable group because they have the self-elected higher calling of being accountable to everyone is a core axiom of "real existing socialism."

The similarities between the socially owned enterprise and the public corporation should not be overdrawn. In particular, the public corporation in the West operates in a market environment often with significant competition from medium-sized or other large firms. It is staffed by people familiar with a private property market economy and is not encumbered by an anti-business ideology. Thus, one would expect a public corporation in the West to be more successful than a generically similar ownership form operating in a bureaucratized anti-business socialist environment.

What is the alternative in the East and in the West to "ownership by everyone and thus by no one"? In the socialist case the alternative is privatization. In the capitalist case the alternative is the "taking private" of a public corporation. In his important article, "The Eclipse of the Public Corporation," Professor Michael Jensen (1989) of the Harvard Business School argued that the leveraged buyout (LBO) movement was replacing the relatively inefficient public corporations with companies privately held by focused groups that recombine ownership and control, such as management teams or LBO associations (for example, Kohlberg Kravis, and Roberts).

Language often seems to control thought. As long as two examples of virtually the same generic phenomenon are described in different vocabularies, it seems difficult to notice the similarities. For instance, the root problem in a socially owned enterprise is referred to in the western literature as a "property rights deficiency" (Furubotn and Pejovich 1974), while the analogous deficiency in the public corporation is called an "agency problem" (Jensen and Meckling 1976). It would be distasteful to recognize a "property rights deficiency" in the predominant economic institution of a private property market economy.

Thus, in the current privatization debates there has been little comparison between the socialist enterprises of the East and the public corporations in the West. Even Professor Jensen neglects to develop the analogy between the taking-private movement in the West and the privatization movement in the East. Conferences on privatization in the American economy witness lengthy discussions of the cost savings from privatizing the laundry for the Pentagon without a word on "privatizing" the Fortune 500. The reason is simple: The companies in the Fortune 500 are already "privately owned."

Given the generic similarity between socially owned enterprises and public corporations, the popular significance of "Wall Street" turns out to be ironic:

> At their best, stockmarkets have many merits: convenience, liquidity, unambiguous prices, low dealing costs. Yet there is another side to them. It has little to do with the drawbacks that are usually attributed to stockmarkets: their periodic volatility,

their indifference to "real values" (whatever those may be), their
gullibility. These alleged defects are, at most, symptoms of a
much deeper malaise, which began with the introduction of
publicly traded shares and has grown ever since: the change in
the meaning of ownership.[1]

It is "Wall Street"—the broad public market in equity shares—
that has dissipated the ownership of public corporations and thus
created the separation of ownership and control. Thus, "Wall
Street" has been the agent of "socialization" quite contrary to its
public image in both the East and West.

This irony is particularly striking in view of an often-proposed
social dividend model of "privatization" that envisages giving each
adult citizen an equal diversified portfolio of shares (or equivalent
vouchers) to instantly create a huge stock market (see below). This
so-called privatization would only create public corporations that
still need to be taken private. There is an old joke that socialism
turned out to be a long road from capitalism to capitalism. Using
the social dividend model, "privatization" might turn out to be the
short road from socialism to socialism.

THE SOCIAL DIVIDEND MODEL OF "PRIVATIZATION"

Variations on the Theme

There are several variations on the social dividend model, but they
all begin by renationalizing all or most socially owned enterprises
to turn them into state-owned enterprises. Then all or most state-
owned enterprises are turned into joint-stock companies with the
shares owned by the state. One distinguishing feature of the variants of the social dividend model is that the net worth represented
by these shares is given away (not sold) as a "social dividend" to
the population. The details of the "social dividend" differ between
the variants.

1. *Equal Corporate Shares*: Equal shares in each company are given
   to each adult citizen.

---

1. "Capitalism: In Triumph, In Flux," *The Economist,* May 5, 1990, 8.

2. *Equal Vouchers*: Each adult citizen is given a voucher (or asset ticket) that can only be used to buy the shares in these companies which are publicly "sold" for the vouchers.
3. *Equal Holding Company Shares*: Controlling shares of industry-related companies (for example, electronics firms) are collected together in holding companies (or mutual funds), and then the shares in the holding companies are distributed equally across the adult population.

Dissipation of Ownership in the Social Dividend Model

One of the main problems in the direct share or voucher versions of the model is that ownership would be dissipated across the entire adult population (a dispersion much greater than the diffused ownership of public corporations in the United States)—so that a company would have no effective private owner. An amusing sidelight of the debate is the assertion that the share/voucher giveaway model does create real private ownership of the shares! That is, of course, true but not very relevant. The point of privatization is to put businesses and not just the ownership of securities into private hands. When the private ownership of a company's stock is spread over the whole population, then the business is, in effect, still socially owned—that is, "owned by everyone and thus by no one."

In an idealized world without transactions costs, it would be possible for an interested party to reconcentrate the ownership of a company through a tender offer for a controlling block of shares. But this is a rather expensive procedure, even in a western economy with a highly efficient stock market. In a country with little history of stock trading and little stock market infrastructure, a tender offer to the entire adult population would be a daunting if not prohibitive undertaking. Even leaving aside the transactions costs, it is also unclear how such a tender offer would be financed. Part of the rationale for the social dividend model is that individuals or small groups do not have the accumulated liquid wealth to buy the shares. If a unified group had the wealth or the borrowing power to finance the purchase of a controlling block of shares, then it would be much more efficient for the state to reserve a control block and sell it. Otherwise, the state could only hope that the market would eventually reassemble enough shares into a control block at an affordable cost in time and resources.

One counter argument is that the U.S. economy seems to function well enough in spite of the separation of ownership and control in the public corporations, so why not just accept the same separation in a "privatization" program in Eastern Europe? The reason is that Eastern Europe does not have the benefit of the same stock of human experience in a market economy. Instead, the managers have the somewhat irrelevant expertise of managing in a socialist firm, and the workers have an accumulated set of "bad habits" from working in a socialist firm. In that environment, dissipated passive ownership of a private firm would soon lead to bankruptcy. If the firm was too large for liquidation to be politically acceptable, then the firm would "bounce back" into the public domain and the citizens would be left holding worthless paper.

The Minority Voucher Model

Some proponents of the social dividend/voucher model admit the dissipation of control in the straight 100 percent model. Hence, the model is modified so that only a minority of the shares of each designated company are to be given away to the citizenry through a voucher system. Then a controlling block of the remaining shares is to be sold by the State Privatization Agency or through the board of directors to an active investor. An unsold portion of shares might be retained by the state as "silent" non-voting shares.

With some variation in the details, this minority voucher model is being seriously investigated in Poland and Czechoslovakia.

This minority giveaway model (with a sold control block) still has two major drawbacks: it dissipates a significant part of the National Patrimony (see below), and it leaves the government with the original problem of selecting the real private owner who will purchase the controlling block of shares.

The retreat from giving away all the shares to giving away only a minority of shares (through vouchers) is not a minor adjustment; it changes the point of the voucher model. In the total voucher model all the ownership is dissipated over the citizenry. In the minority voucher model the original problem of determining the real private owner has yet to be solved. The real privatization only comes when the State Privatization Agency (or the board of directors) sells the controlling block of shares to a private buyer. Because the minority voucher model is silent on the original question of determining the controlling private owner, it is not itself a privatization model. It is a method of lowering the price on the controlling block of shares to be privatized—while winning political favor for the government through the giveaway.

The minority voucher model leaves the same menu of options for the real privatization. Is the controlling block to be sold to foreign interests, to the managers and workers through a leveraged buyout, or to some other buyer?

Dissipation of the National Patrimony in the Social Dividend Model

One of the main problems with the partial or total giveaway of shares is that the state gets no sorely needed cash from unloading its enterprises. The pressing public needs of the post-communist governments include:

1. meeting interest and principal payments on foreign debt;
2. funding a social safety net and retraining programs for workers who become unemployed as a result of the economic restructuring;
3. financing pensions and health care needs of an aging population;
4. modernizing the educational system for the new challenges facing youth;
5. paying for needed environmental cleanups and safeguards; and
6. rebuilding the infrastructure needed for a modern economy.

The free-transfer model might prove to be an overwhelming temptation for politicians who are quite willing to postpone financing public needs in return for a burst of political support in these times of difficult restructuring. As in the case of the British privatizations with partial giveaways (sale of shares with discounts), most citizens are quite willing to resell the shares, reap the capital gains, and go on a consumption binge. This would be particularly true with the levels of pent-up consumption demand in Eastern Europe.

The Holding Company Variation

The holding company variation counteracts the dissolution of control by allocating the shares to a small number of holding companies (or mutual funds) with a controlling block for each company held in a single holding company. Perhaps the firms from the same industry would be collected together in a holding company (for example, electronics firms) so that the management and staff of the holding company could develop an industry-specific expertise. The shares of the holding companies are then distributed gratis across the adult population.

The main problem with the holding company variant is that it seems to be a pseudo-privatization. The holding companies are essentially the industrial ministries of state socialism, except that they are organized at one remove as joint-stock companies. The holding companies provide a well-defined owner for each enterprise, but then so do the founding ministries of state socialism.

The distribution of holding company shares across the population is only a distribution of wealth claims into private hands (like giving out government bonds), not a privatization of industry. Firms would not be managed by owners, but by agents answerable to holding company managers who are again agents "answerable" to the population at large or answerable to the ministers in the government's State Privatization Agency. Thus, instead of managers having private ownership, they are agents of agents of the general public.

Perhaps it is a sign of the infancy of the privatization debate that the holding company variation with managers as agents of agents of the public is even considered as a form of "privatization" of industry. The real privatization would only come as the holding companies/ministries sold off the operating companies. In the meantime, the enterprises would be in a "holding pattern" while the government tried to decide where they would ultimately land.

Thus, the holding company variation—like the minority voucher model—looks like a pseudo-privatization that would buy time by postponing the real privatization and would give a political shot-in-the-arm to the government from the free distribution of shares.

CAPITAL MARKET ARGUMENTS FOR THE SOCIAL DIVIDEND MODEL

Interested Owners: Active or Passive?

Some other arguments for the social dividend model are based on capital market considerations. The principal argument is that the social dividend would instantly create a capital market of interested owners, which is necessary for the efficient allocation of capital.

One minor problem with this argument is the presumption that it is important to have "interested owners" independent of whether the owners are active or passive. Unfortunately, the social dividend model only creates a broad class of interested but passive stockholders. Each citizen would hold only a miniscule portion of the shares of a company. Transaction costs would prohibit any concerted and coordinated effort by the citizen-shareholders, even assuming they had the relevant information.

The reserved control block variation would create an interested and active owner, but precisely because the controlling block of equity was not given away as a social dividend. The control block model is based on the admission that the broad distribution of securities to create a capital market would not create an active owner.

Capital Market Valuation and Efficiency Arguments

Quite aside from the question of active or passive owners, proponents of the social dividend model argue that:

1. The model instantly creates a broad public market in equity shares.
2. A capital market is necessary for the valuation of capital.

3. The valuation of capital is necessary for the efficient allocation of capital.

Thus, it is argued that a broad public market for equity shares is necessary for the efficient allocation of capital. This argument seems to contain several interesting flaws. One must first differentiate between two rather different types of "capital markets": the market for physical capital (for example, capital goods such as machinery) and financial capital (for example, loanable funds and debt securities) and the public market for equity shares.

To clearly see the difference, consider a private enterprise market economy in which all corporations were privately held (for example, where privately held firms were not taken public, and where all public corporations had been taken private). In such a genuinely privatized market economy there would be no public market for equity shares, but there would be the usual markets for physical and financial capital. There would also be the "market" for private placements of equity shares. Private placements are individually negotiated sales of shares usually based on valuations by accredited valuators (because there is no public market giving a share value).

The argument cited above that a broad public market in equity shares is necessary for the efficient allocation of capital would imply that such a genuinely privatized market economy was inefficient. We shall argue not only that the implication is false, but that the privatized market economy would more efficiently utilize capital than an economy with corporate ownership spread throughout a public equity market.

To evaluate the argument in detail, consider a capital allocation decision within a firm. An investment of capital, a capital project, is being considered—say, the purchase of a new machine. Management must decide if the project is worthwhile. The analysis of the capital project requires knowing:

1. the purchase price and transportation/installation costs of the machine;
2. the costs to finance the purchase of the machine;
3. the costs of running the machine over its economic lifetime;

4. the costs of the labor and the inputs necessary to operate the machine; and

5. the projected demand and selling price of the outputs produced using the machine over its lifetime.

With this information the discounted present value of the capital project could be estimated to determine if the project was worthwhile (positive net present value).

We are now in a position to see which capital markets are necessary for the efficient allocation of capital. In particular, the analysis of a capital project requires knowing the costs of the physical capital (for example, the price of the machine) and the costs of financial capital (for example, the interest rate at which money could be borrowed to undertake the project). But the analysis does not require any market valuation of the equity shares of the firm considering the investment (or of the firms that produce the machines or loan the money). The efficient allocation of capital thus seems to require capital markets in physical or financial capital but it does not require a capital market in the sense of a public market in equity shares.

This analysis confirms the suspicion of a flaw in the argument that privately held companies are inherently inefficient allocators of capital because they lack publicly traded equity shares. Indeed, the opposite seems to be the case. When control is separated from ownership through the dispersion of publicly traded shares, then capital investment decisions are made by managers who are not investing their own capital. The results are predictable. By dispersing ownership in public corporations, the stock market itself leads to the inefficient use of capital.

Risk-Allocative Efficiency

There is, however, another way that a public market in shares might contribute to efficiency in this case: risk-allocative efficiency. If a hundred risk adverse individuals can pool their (statistically independent) risks, then each can obtain almost the same average return with a greatly reduced variance, so that everyone is better off and no one is worse off. Thus, the original situation of unpooled risks was not efficient.

There are two quite distinct and even opposing ways in which risk-bearing can affect efficiency. Those people who by their efforts can affect the performance of a firm (for example, managers and workers) need to bear much of the risks of poor performance in order to have the incentive to put forth their best effort. Poor effort due to insufficient exposure to risk is an example of "moral hazard." Poor incentive structures induce "X-inefficiency" (Leibenstein 1976, 1987). Thus, some risk-bearing on the part of effort-relevant people is necessary for efficiency. But, as noted above, risk-bearing can also lead to risk-allocative inefficiency.

The design of an efficient firm must proceed along several interconnected dimensions. Risk-allocative efficiency and effort-efficiency (or X-efficiency) must be considered in addition to the allocative efficiency that is facilitated by competitive commodity markets.

The relevant point for our present argument is that privatized owner-operated firms without any publicly traded equity might not be efficient from the risk-allocative viewpoint. Perhaps some risks could be shared with outsiders who could pool risks without unduly dampening the incentives for the owners to put forth their best efforts.

Risk sharing with outsiders, however, does not require a public market in equity shares. The risk sharing could be accomplished with a public market in variable-return non-voting securities. Because these securities would be non-voting, the variable return should be mandatory (as opposed to discretionary). Variable-interest debentures and participating bonds are examples of such securities.

Could there be a large public market in such variable-return non-voting securities? It is interesting to note that the widely dispersed equity shares in public corporations already function almost in that manner. The small shareholder buys shares for their income features, not for the votes. Management in public corporations buys the acquiescence of the shareholders with regular (that is, quasi-mandatory) dividends. The "missed dividend" carries more information than the "made dividend" in large public corporations.

This observation raises the logical question: Why continue to "play the game" that far-flung shareholders of public companies are the real "owners"? Because the shares function as de facto non-voting participating bonds, why not legally turn them into such securities (as occurs when junk bonds are substituted for equity in a leveraged buyout)? Perhaps the answer is that such a transformation would raise the awkward question of who should then be the real owners of the public corporations. And that is the question analogous to the privatization question now facing the post-communist economies. But in this case there would be no illusion that the public companies would be "privatized" by a wide dispersion of the equity shares (because the privately owned shares are already widely dispersed).

ACTIVE OWNERSHIP: A MISSING INGREDIENT IN THE PRIVATIZATION DEBATE

We have argued that not all "privatization" is privatization; not all "ownership" is (active) ownership. But what is active ownership, and how is it differentiated from the nominal passive ownership of a company?

The distinction between active and passive ownership is related to the notions of X-efficiency (or effort-efficiency) and effort-relevance. Ownership of a company (that is, ownership of equity shares) includes the rights to the net income and the control rights (for example, the voting rights to elect the directors). A person is "effort-relevant" to a company if an increase or decrease in the person's motivation and effort can affect the operations and net income of the company. A person's ownership rights in a company represent "passive ownership" if the person is not effort-relevant to the company. In contrast, active ownership is ownership in the hands of effort-relevant people.

One major example of passive ownership is the "ownership by all the people" in a socialist country (even though this ownership is not legally packaged in equity shares). As argued by Berle and Means (1932, 1968), the major western example of passive ownership is the ownership of the public corporations, the corporations with widely dispersed and publicly traded shares.

We have pointed out the analogies between the state or socially owned enterprises of the East and the public corporations of the West even though the latter are said to be "privately owned." The similarities based on passive ownership outweigh the differences in legal terminology.

If privatization in post-communist societies is to be a genuine change in ownership, then it should be more than just a change from a public form of passive ownership to a private form of passive ownership. The purpose of privatization should be to replace passive-public ownership with active-private ownership.

In a recent survey on capitalism, *The Economist* developed the related distinction between "punter capitalism," with companies in the hands of passive shareholders who are only spectators betting on the company from the sidelines, and "proprietor capitalism," with companies in the hands of active owners.[2]

The principal means of converting punter capitalism back into proprietor capitalism has been the leveraged buyout movement which *The Economist* described as "the most remarkable change in capitalism since the creation of the stockmarket" (12).

From the viewpoint of X-efficiency, equity ownership in the hands of effort-irrelevant people is "wasted ownership." They can only be punters, spectators betting on the outcome of the race. There may be non-efficiency reasons to distribute wealth (for example, cash or debt securities) from a company to people who are not effort-relevant to the company (for example, past employees). But it is a wasted opportunity to "incentivize" with equity shares those people who can have no effect on the company. On the other hand, it is also a wasted opportunity not to incentivize with equity those who can by their efforts have an effect on the company.

Thus, from the viewpoint of X-efficiency or effort-efficiency, it is best to associate equity ownership with, and only with, effort-relevance to the company. Equity shares in the hands of a person otherwise unconnected to a company is wasted ownership; a person working in a company but without shares is a wasted opportunity.

What are the lessons for the privatization debate in post-communists economies? One central lesson is that for the X-efficient correlation of ownership with effort, the model of privatization

2. *Op. cit*, 5–20.

should not be the public flotation of shares (as in the U.K.), much less the free transfer of shares to the public of the social dividend model. Leaving aside the sale of company to a foreign buyer, the principal form of privatization that creates active (private) ownership is the form used in the United States to take private a public corporation, namely the manager/worker leveraged buyout.

MANAGER/WORKER LEVERAGED BUYOUTS

What is a manager/worker LBO? First of all, the "B" in LBO stands for "buy." An LBO is not a giveaway. The managers and workers are buying the assets or shares of the previous state-owned, socially owned, or public enterprise; it is not "given" to the workers. Some governments (for example, the Markovic government of Yugoslavia) have suggested a system of worker discounts to be applied for the purchase of shares. Worker discounts are consistent with a manager/worker LBO, but it is not a necessary component of the LBO idea. Indeed, inappropriate objections are sometimes made to the LBO model because of a confusion with various worker-oriented giveaway schemes.

Secondly, it is a "leveraged" buyout in the sense that the financing of the buyout is collateralized by the purchased asset and the earning power generated using the asset. The managers and workers do not need to have the personal wealth to finance the deal. Their homes, cars, or personal assets are not collateral. The earning power of the company itself stands behind the loans needed to fund the transaction.

It might also be noted that some of the credit for the transaction might be supplied by the seller. The seller might take some "paper" instead of being paid entirely in cash. The "paper" might be a term note to be paid off over a period of years or it might be some form of debt-equity hybrid indicating continued participation by the seller in the company.

For financial and motivational viewpoint, the managers and workers should also put up some of the finance out of pocket. Experience with worker ownership in America and elsewhere shows that personal financial investment is a strong bonding or commitment mechanism to align the interests of the worker with the long-term interests of the company.

Most enterprises being privatized are overstaffed. Some workers can be spun off in segments or in new small businesses sponsored by "internal incubators" set up inside the enterprise. But eventually a filtering mechanism may be required to determine which managers and workers will belong to the privatized company. The willingness to make a personal investment, particularly with personal credit available from local sources, is an obvious filter mechanism.

If third-party credit from financial institutions, seller-supplied credit, and manager/worker financial investment are insufficient to finance a buyout, then a foreign joint venture partner might be brought into the deal to complete the financial package.

Thirdly, a manager-/worker-owned company is a particular form of private ownership. It should not be confused with the form of social ownership known as "worker self-management" in Yugoslavia and other Eastern European countries. The most developed and implemented form of the manager/worker LBO is the American employee stock ownership plan (ESOP). Even though ESOPs were only introduced in 1973, today over 11 percent of the industrial workforce in America work in companies with partial or complete employee ownership through ESOPs. Because ESOP companies are privately owned joint-stock companies, it is rather implausible to associate ESOPs with the socialist "self-managed" firms and to criticize them on that basis. An example of an ESOP-type manager/worker LBO is outlined in Appendix 9-2.

We believe the manager/worker LBOs offer many advantages over other models of genuine privatization (for more documentation, see Wright et al. 1989). From the X-efficiency viewpoint, it fulfills the ideal of active private ownership, because ownership is associated with effort-relevant people—the managers and workers of the enterprise. Absentee passive ownership is effort-irrelevant ownership, which thus sacrifices an opportunity for increased X-efficiency.

In addition, the LBO model offers a method to elicit and reward the entrepreneurial talent latent in the ranks of existing top and middle management. Not every attempt to organize and finance a manager/worker LBO will be successful. Some managers will not have the talent or will not inspire enough confidence to organize and lead the buyout effort in the first place. Others will make an attempt but will fail to raise the necessary money. Some deals will require foreign joint venture partners, but the current management might be rejected by the potential partners. Thus, the LBO model has a built-in market-driven process to select the best managers for the privatized enterprises. This selection process stands in sharp contrast to models where selection of the enterprise managers and board members would be part of the patronage controlled by the holding companies, ministries, or the State Privatization Agency.

A DECENTRALIZED PRIVATIZATION STRATEGY

The LBO model for privatization goes hand in hand with a decentralized model for the whole privatization process (the so-called privatization from below). Much of the privatization debate seems to assume that the central privatization agency of the government, the State Privatization Agency, must negotiate and execute each genuine privatization deal (the so-called privatization from above). The impossibly slow pace of this procedure has generated some of the pressure for the pseudo-privatization plans such as the share/voucher giveaways and the holding company schemes. Yet there is an alternative that fosters genuine privatization, a decentralized privatization process emphasizing the LBO model where:

1. The LBO privatization deals are self-executing according to the rules established by the government.
2. Organizing LBO privatization deals becomes a new private industry facilitated by investment banking and management consulting firms.
3. The government's Privatization Agency operates as the regulatory agency for this new "privatization industry" which enforces the rules governing the privatization deals and ultimately receives the net worth of the enterprises being privatized.

Heretofore the most notorious examples of decentralized privatizations have been the unregulated "spontaneous privatizations" occurring in Hungary and Poland. Managers of socially owned companies have taken advantage of the lack of serious regulations concerning deal structure and valuation to arrange "sweet deals" for themselves and foreign joint venture partners.

Instead of stopping all decentralized privatizations, the governments of Eastern Europe should use the experience with spontaneous privatizations to draw up adequate regulations. Any government trying to foster a market economy should seek to regulate, not abolish, spontaneous economic initiatives. What principles might guide the regulations for a decentralized privatization process?

The first principle is that managers, workers, or other buyers should ultimately pay the government (for example, a privatization agency or fund) or some other designated social entity the full value of the assets acquired from the state or from "society."

This full-payment principle should be decoupled from the question of the final disposition of the social value. That value might be used to pay off foreign debt, to fund pension plans, to pay for the social safety net, or to rebuild the infrastructure. Worker-share discount schemes tend to confuse the two purposes. Past employees might have a valid claim on part of the accumulated net worth of an enterprise, but the distribution of part of that value to them in the form of discounted equity shares in the privatized company would be wasted ownership.

Another question is: "Full payment for what?" A favorite valuation formula in the West is the discounted present value of all future free cash flows of the enterprise. But this assumes that the state owns and is selling the full profit potential of the privatized company. Yet that claim is implausible, because the state, ex hypothesis, cannot generate the profits of the privatized companies. The attempt to value at full profit potential is also imprudent, because it would remove the incentive from the private buyers.

What is the alternative? The state in fact is selling the net assets of the enterprise accumulated in the past, not the economic profits generated by the future private company. Thus, the lower bound on valuation should be the net value of the assets under conditions of orderly liquidation (because an orderly liquidation is the alternative to a sale of the company). The upper bound of the valuation is the "replacement value" in the sense of what the potential buyer would have to pay for plant and equipment of equal utility to the existing assets. That is the realistic upper bound, because the potential buyer always has the option of purchasing such an alternative plant and employing the requisite managers and workers from the old enterprise. Indeed, many foreign investors are already showing a preference for constructing new plants to avoid hidden future costs that might attach to existing enterprises.

One other point about valuations in the context of privatization is that the valuation is not an end in itself. It is only a means to the end of privatizing the enterprise in a manner that is fair to the buyer and seller. The need for a definitive valuation can be altogether finessed by using contingent variable pricing on the transaction. In the mergers and acquisition business in the West, when the buyer and seller put irreconcilably different valuations on an enterprise, then the transaction might still be completed using a variable pricing arrangement known as an "earn-out." The future payments are contingent on the profits made by the enterprise over a multi-year period. The same sort of contingently priced transactions can be used to bypass the lack of reliable valuation information in privatization deals.

Given the demonstrated potential for subpar valuations and other improprieties in spontaneous privatizations, the government's Privatization Agency must have the power to block any proposed self-privatization LBO deal. If the Agency has been officially notified of a proposed deal and does not object within a set time period (say, thirty days), then the deal may be completed. That is an implicit approval mechanism. Alternatively, an explicit approval by the Agency within a certain time period might be required to complete the transaction. With either an implicit or explicit approval mechanism, the contrast is with a centralized privatization strategy where the Agency (or subsidiary holding companies) would negotiate and execute each deal.

If the Agency objects to a proposed transaction, then there should be a set procedure that must be followed before a new transaction can be submitted for approval. If the disapproval is based on valuation considerations, then the procedure should require that the company pay for another valuation by an Agency-appointed valuator. There could also be a mandatory time period that must pass before a new submission. To avoid the expense of a new valuation and the costly wait, it is in the interests of the buyout group to make sure that the original proposal is supported by one or more credible valuations by independent professional valuators.

A proposal might be objectionable for non-valuation reasons such as the cash portion of the deal. For instance, although the valuation might be generous, it was to be paid off in twenty-year notes to the seller. The Agency would require a larger upfront cash component in the payment schedule.

There are a number of ways to expedite the approval of the transactions. The Agency should publish a set of models or templates for the structure of the transactions. A proposed deal should use one of the models or risk a lengthy approval process. Another idea is for the buyout group to invite some respected business or financial expert to participate in the negotiations involved in preparing the deal. That should heighten the credibility of the proposed transaction and expedite the approval process. Multiple valuations in rough agreement with each other would, of course, help to substantiate the assumed net asset value. Uninvolved investment banks might be hired to give fairness opinions about the proposed transaction.

A final problem is to delimit the privatization transactions. For instance, when a socially owned company sells something to a private company, that could be a normal commercial transaction. But the private company might be set up by the managers of the socially owned company, and the managers might be selling the operating assets to their private company at knockdown prices. In that case, it should be classified as a privatization transaction and brought under the purview of the Agency. Thus, the sale of substantial social- or state-owned operating assets to a private company should be classified as a "privatization transaction." Unreported privatization transactions between social and private entities would run the risk of being unwound in addition to fines and penalties.

With appropriate guidelines and regulations, the Privatization Agency could oversee and govern a decentralized process of widespread privatization based on the LBO and related models. Instead of the "single-file" negotiation of deals by one or more government agencies, hundreds of deals could be prepared simultaneously by the market-driven privatization industry operating under the regulatory authority of the Privatization Agency.

APPENDIX 9-1: DO THE POST-COMMUNIST GOVERNMENTS REALLY WANT PRIVATIZATION NOW?

One of the surprising developments in the privatization debate in Eastern Europe is the emergence within the democratically elected post-communist governments of significant forces against short-term privatization. In the short run these forces favor the renationalization and state administration (perhaps through holding companies) of most companies of any size. There are differences of opinion within the non-privatization camp about the eventual disposition of the companies, but that question is postponed comfortably beyond the operational planning horizon of the government.

Many of the positions in the privatization debate are hard to understand without appreciating this emerging anti-privatization (or, at least, non-privatization) sentiment. Many of the arguments against a particular privatization strategy turn out after further analysis and debate to be based on sentiments against any (genuine) form of privatization.

What are the origins of the non-privatization views? One common argument uses the process of elimination; all the possible candidates as private owners are unacceptable. Foreign ownership of important companies is politically unpalatable. Wealthy domestic buyers are rejected because they are likely to be either *nomenklatura* or black-market speculators. Returning emigres with enough wealth to buy companies are an exception to this rule, but they can only account for a minute fraction of the companies.

The leaders of the democratically elected anti-communist governments have often spent the years of communist rule in external exile or in some form of internal exile clearly outside the power structure of government and industry. When elected to power, some tend to view all enterprise managers as being *nomenklatura* or, at least, communist collaborators, even though such views may, with a few clear exceptions, be decades out of date (for example, in

Slovenia and Croatia). Hence, some new leaders tend to reject any form of privatization, such as manager/worker leveraged buyouts, which would not necessarily involve a wholesale change in management. It will take years to develop a new management elite, so in the meantime the "non-privatizers" argue that the government must maintain or reassert custodianship over the enterprises.

Some opposition to manager/worker LBOs is based on the element of worker ownership. Some government officials and privatization advisers use a strong rhetoric in favor of the increased "efficiency" of having ownership in private hands. But their concrete proposals tend toward the social dividend model, which diffuses ownership in the hands of the effort-irrelevant general population of the country. In spite of the rhetoric about efficiency and privatization, they are against anything more than token ownership of an enterprise by the one well-defined effort-relevant set of private individuals: the people working in the enterprise.

Some opposition to the manager/worker LBO model of privatization seems to be based on valid arguments against something quite different, the socially owned "self-managed" firms of Eastern Europe. This suggests that some commentators may simply be unfamiliar with manager/worker LBOs in the West such as the American ESOP.

Another argument is that managers and workers should not have significant ownership because that would make the firm less attractive to foreign investors. Of course, for a given investment, a foreign investor would rather have 100 percent than 70 percent or 49 percent, regardless of whether the other ownership was by workers and managers, the government, or other investors. However, foreign investors who are making a long-term investment (as opposed to asset-strippers) would probably want to have the workers on their side rather than in opposition. Partial employee ownership, as in the American ESOP, works to align the basic economic interests of the workers in parallel with the interests of other owners. Moreover, the ESOP structure aligns the economic interests of the workers with the firm on a long-term basis. As the workforce turns over, the exiting workers are cashed out over a period of years, and the entering workers earn their way into co-ownership.

In the absence of plausible arguments, opposition to western-style employee ownership may turn out to be little more than a thinly disguised class bias against workers as the "wrong sort of people" to have private ownership. Such attitudes will not help private enterprise market economies to become firmly rooted in the post-communist societies.

The people whose land and/or companies were expropriated under communist rule are another source of non-privatization sentiment. Political parties representing these former property owners are often well represented in the democratically elected coalitions. Any genuine privatization program would put an end to their hopes of getting back their former land or company. On the other hand, any government that contemplated giving back specific land or companies to previous owners could not at the same time implement a coherent privatization program. Property titles would be clouded by the possibility of future legal action by those who were or who claimed to be the previous owners or their descendants.

A coherent privatization program should be decoupled from any program to partially rectify some well-established injustices through wealth transfers (for example, government bonds) perhaps financed by the proceeds of the privatization sell-offs. But much of the current political sentiment seems focused on returning the specific assets to the prior owners or their descendants, and that is another political force against any alternative. But since that political force is not dominant, its default strategy is public ownership because that does not foreclose the future option of distribution to prior owners.

A minor source of anti-privatization opinion is the traditional attitude (shorn of Marxist overtones) that thinks the conduct of private business elicits only the baser human motives. Any proposed privatization transaction is viewed as the unseemly attempt of the buyer to "feather his own nest" at the expense of the "public good." To further complicate matters, the borderline between healthy self-interest and unhealthy "insider trading" is almost completely uncharted in Eastern Europe. Thus, some newly elected guardians of the "public good" seem to object to any specific privatization buyout transactions and have no concrete guidelines to propose for the privatization process. The alternative is to maintain or reassert public ownership so that the enterprises can be administered by the "pure-hearted" for the "public good."

Lastly, a source of anti-privatization sentiment is the "drive for power," which has not gone out of fashion with the demise of communism. After years of struggle and finally coming to power, the new leaders will naturally want to augment their power and patronage. Privatization would have the opposite effect by removing the selection of enterprise boards and management from the government (or its holding companies) and by creating independent centers of social power.

We have outlined some of the forces within the new anti-communist governments of Eastern Europe that operate to stall or reverse the trend toward privatization. Without understanding these forces, it would be difficult to appreciate the appeal of various schemes of renationalization and pseudo-privatization (for example, the holding company scheme).

APPENDIX 9-2: EXAMPLE OF A PRIVATIZATION USING AN ESOP-TYPE LBO

An ESOP with internal worker shareholding in the form of "partner capital accounts" can be written into the Constitution or bylaws of any joint-stock company. Such an ESOP built into the structure of the company is called an "internal ESOP." Consider the balance sheet in Table 9-1 of a socially owned enterprise prior to privatization.

The socially owned firm starts off with social capital of US$60 million. The company is converted into a joint-stock company with an initial US$60 million worth of shares issued. The business plan calls for an additional US$22 million of working capital and new capital equipment. A privatization transaction is proposed with a foreign venture partner to bring in US$40 million. The managers and workers initially raise US$10 million in cash from their own sources. A western bank agrees to extend an eight-year loan for US$15 million through the ESOP (as if it was a loan to the workers and managers to buy new shares).

Table 9-1. Initial Balance Sheet of Socially Owned Enterprise

Assets	Liabilities
US$80 mm	US$20 mm - Debt
	US$60 mm - Social Capital

The company pays off an ESOP loan over a period of years with pension-like payments that are treated as company expenses.

Thus, the total capital raised so far is:

US$15 mm = Bank Loan to ESOP
US$40 mm = Foreign Direct Investment
US$10 mm = Worker and Manager Equity

$65 mm = Capital Raised So Far

The capital needs are:

$22 mm = New Working Capital and Investment,
$60 mm = Social Capital to be Transferred to the
                  Privatization Agency to "Buy" Private Firm

$82 mm = Capital needed for privatization and restructuring

The "capital gap" is US$17 million (= 82 - 65), which could come from the Privatization Agency as an example of seller-supplied credit. Being impressed by the money raised by the managers and workers, the Agency considered two ways to supply the credit:

1. hold US$17 million in preferred shares to be bought back by the private firm over a ten-year period, or
2. extend a US$17 million credit to the internal ESOP.

There is a sizable difference between the options to the work-force and the joint venture partner. Without the US$17 million, the joint venture partner holds a majority position—US$40 million versus US$25 million (10 + 15) held by the workers and managers. If the Agency holds the US$17 million in preferred stock, the relative positions of the joint venture partner and the workforce will remain the same as the firm buys back the preferred stock. But if the US$17 million credit is extended to the ESOP, it is as if the workforce had borrowed the money and bought voting stock with it. Then the workforce (workers and managers) have US$42 million (25 + 17) equity for majority control.

After some lobbying, the Agency extends the additional US$17 million of credit (subordinated to the bank debt) to the internal ESOP to purchase US$17 million of shares in the name of the workforce. The original US$60 million share issue is supplemented by a US$22 million new issue. Thus, in Table 9-2, the balance sheet after the transaction is shown:

As the ESOP debt is paid off, that value accrues to the worker-partner capital accounts in the internal ESOP. The Agency received US$10 million cash from the workers and managers, US$33 million cash from JV capital injection in the firm, and a US$17 million note from the company. Thus, the net effect is that the original social capital of US$60 million was transferred to the Agency.

This example presupposes no worker discounts for the purchase of equity, but it can be modified to illustrate the combined effect of an ESOP and worker discounts. Consider the worker discounts suggested by Prime Minister Markovic of Yugoslavia. Suppose there are 500 workers and managers with an average of twenty years on the job and an average pay of US$600 a month. If the workers are allowed a 2 percent discount per year up to three years of pay, then they have a 40 percent discount on share purchases up to 3 x 12 months x US$600 = US$21,600. Thus, the discount is worth 40 percent of US$21,600, or US$8,640. To buy US$10 million of shares, the average worker must supply US$10 million/500 = US$20,000, which is less than the maximum discountable purchase of US$21,600. With the 40 percent discount, the average worker needs to pay US$12,000 in cash over a period of years. Assuming the government would allow ten years' financing with a 20

Table 9-2. Balance Sheet of Privatized Enterprise

Assets	Liabilities
$80 mm	$20 mm = Debt
$22 mm	$17 mm = ESOP Agency Debt
	$15 mm = ESOP Bank Debt
	$40 mm = Foreign Equity
	$10 mm = Internal ESOP

percent down payment, the average worker would have to pay US$2,400 in cash now and have US$960 deducted from his or her pay each year for ten years. After all the ESOP and personal loans were paid off, the average worker's capital account would be worth US$84,000 (= 42/82 x US$82 million/500) with no additional profits (or losses).

REFERENCES

Berle, Adolf, and Gardiner Means. 1932. *The Modern Corporation and Private Property*. New York: Macmillan.

———. 1968. *The Modern Corporation and Private Property* (Revised Edition). New York: Harcourt, Brace and World.

Furubotn, E., and S. Pejovich. 1974. *The Economics of Property Rights*. Cambridge: Ballinger Publishing Company.

Jensen, Michael C. 1989. "Eclipse of the Public Corporation." *Harvard Business Review*, no. 5, (September–October): 61–74.

Jensen, Michael C., and William H. Meckling. 1976. "Theory of the Firm: Managerial Behavior, Agency Costs and Ownership Structure." *Journal of Financial Economics* 3, 4 (October): 305–60.

Leibenstein, Harvey. 1976. *Beyond Economic Man*. Cambridge, Mass.: Harvard University Press.

———— 1987. *Inside the Firm: The Inefficiencies of Hierarchy.* Cambridge, Mass.: Harvard University Press.

Wright, M., R. S. Thompson, and K. Robbie. 1989. "Privatisation via Management and Employee Buyouts: Analysis and U.K. Experience." *Annals of Public and Cooperative Economics* 4, 60: 399–429.

Part II

Working Group Reports

10

Working Group 1:
German Reunification

David B. Audretsch

When the Berlin Wall came down on November 9, 1989, a fundamental and inevitable economic, political, and social revolution began. The Wall was built to serve four functions: (1) to insulate the East German economy from lower-priced and more desirable Western goods and services; (2) to block any erosion of its investment in human capital through the emigration of educated and trained workers to the West; (3) to prevent subsidized low-priced staples, such as bread, from being shipped to the West; and (4) to choke off alternate opportunities for workers, producers, and consumers. Without the Wall, East Germany's forty-year history as a planned centralized economy would never have been possible.

The East German government's decision to centralize economic assets on a massive scale was an attempt to facilitate centralized planning and to exploit scale economies beyond anything imaginable in Western democracies. Competition was effectively stamped out and centralization was promoted. By 1989 there were only 224 giant *kombinate* (combines), each a centrally administered monopoly. Managerial methods became paralyzed and disastrously immune to further progress because of these monopolistic combines and the absence of a competitive market. As long as the Wall remained in place and the economy was insulated from foreign competition, the system remained viable. The standard of living, however, continued to slip behind that of the West, and at an alarming and ever-increasing rate.

The opening of the Berlin Wall left entire economic structures, agents, and institutions exposed. Not only were Western consumer goods and assets available with hard currency at sometimes incredibly attractive prices, but unprecedented numbers of workers, particularly the most educated and skilled, began flocking westward in search of higher wages. By further eliminating barriers to free capital and labor flows, Germany's economic and monetary union on July 1, 1990, inevitably accelerated the reduction of price and wage differentials between East and West. Movement toward a new equilibrium has begun.

West and East Germany must now confront two fundamental questions. First, which path should be pursued in order to ensure economic and political survival in the difficult transition from a centrally planned to a market economy? Second, which, if any, socialist traditions and institutions should be preserved, and which West German institutions and practices should be resisted? These same questions apply to other Eastern European countries as well. Their solutions, however, may not. Germany's political and economic union has given West Germany a serious stake in East Germany's successful transition to a capitalist economy and has thus guaranteed the East German economy substantial financial assistance and unusual opportunities for integration into the Western economy. For these reasons and many others, the East German "takeover" model is inappropriate for other Eastern European countries. Nevertheless, there are at least elements of this model that can be usefully applied by all Eastern reformers, and the following recommendations incorporate them.

Privatization of State-Controlled Assets

1. Some form of auction should be used to facilitate asset valuation and the privatization of existing state-owned assets.
2. A minimal acceptable price (to be determined by the *Treuhandanstalt*, the German government agency overseeing privatization) will be enforced in order to prevent "fire sale" sell-offs.
3. Auctions will sell either small bundles or individual plants, depending on the recommendation of the *Treuhandanstalt* or an analogous institution.

4. Privatization in Eastern Europe should proceed along a more
    gradual and longer time trajectory than through an instanta-
    neous shock. This will provide some stability during the tran-
    sition period.

Adaptation of Antitrust Laws and Injection of Competition

1. Private monopolies should not be allowed to replace public
    ones. Individual firms should be actively prevented from dom-
    inating entire industries.
2. In order to inject competition from foreign firms, tariff and
    nontariff trade barriers should not be applied.
3. Important exceptions where such trade barriers may deserve
    serious consideration are infant industries or promising key
    products that have been targeted for preferential treatment.

Creation of an Economic Environment
Favorable to Foreign Investment

1. Labor and social policies should prevent an increase in wages
    that exceeds the rate of productivity growth.
2. While a safety net is essential to contain potential public un-
    rest, social benefits should not match those of Western neigh-
    bors until there is productivity parity.
3. The state must assume responsibility for all old enterprise
    debts.
4. State-initiated environmental clean-up must begin immedi-
    ately, and firm liability made explicit.
5. Across-the-board adaptation of legal infrastructure should be
    completed immediately to eliminate confusion over copyrights,
    liability, and torts.

Removal of Governmental and Legal Barriers

1. In order to maximize employment growth and innovation,
    legislation should be enacted to encourage entrepreneurial ac-

tivity and the creation of new firms (as opposed to a mere re-structuring of existing state-owned combines).

2. A decentralized and dispersed financial system rather than a concentrated structure of financial institutions should be established to facilitate new-venture financing. Eastern European financial institutions must use their knowledge of local conditions to become established in the international capital market and to channel funds into their domestic economies.

3. New small and medium-sized firms should be granted lower tax rates, higher depreciation allowances, and subsidized interest loans to promote entrepreneurial activity.

Creation of a College and Institutional Consortium to Promote the Exchange, Development and Rapid Spread of New Ideas

1. The consortium will be a clearinghouse for new and original ideas, will identify and bring together experts from East and West, will facilitate and coordinate their findings at regular conferences, and will distribute the results internationally.

2. Discussions will focus on managerial techniques, business legislation, market behavior, and technological know-how.

3. In addition, the consortium will work with private businesses and state agencies to coordinate a management training program, combined with on-the-job training for middle- and upper-level Eastern European managers.

A New U.S. Eastern European Development Agency Should Be Established to Disseminate Knowledge, Funds, and Technical Assistance

1. These responsibilities are currently under the aegis of a single state employee. Funding and additional staff are essential.

2. This agency's activities should be actively coordinated with those of the consortium and should include frequent joint conferences.

3. Membership should be expanded to include other Western countries to widen the funding base.

11

Working Group 2:
Eastern European Reform

Kalman Mizsei and Jenik Radon

Privatization is the restructuring of a state- or government-owned economy on a commercial and non-state or private basis. In addition to state enterprises, state-owned entities to be privatized could include state-controlled or -directed cooperatives and communal properties.

Privatization should be designed to increase capital investment, to create a self-sustaining middle class through the establishment of small and medium-sized firms, to reduce the size and the influence the state sector, and to break up existing monopolies. These changes will require the creation or development of a Western-style financial infrastructure that would include a modern banking system with varied financial instruments, such as mutual and pension funds, and a supporting organizational infrastructure, that is, stock exchange, brokerages, et cetera.

Privatization should help create a self-sustaining private sector and reduce, to the extent reasonable, the outstanding indebtedness of an economy.

As the economies of Czechoslovakia, Hungary, and Poland are poorly developed and relatively depressed, it is essential that privatization proceed as rapidly as possible to increase their standard of living to a level comparable to that of the European Common Market countries. To the extent feasible, privatization should treat all citizens of a country equitably and fairly.

Given the urgency of converting these economies, implementation may require radical changes. Because of the heterogeneity of their cultures and populations, unique and varied methods must be employed.

STRATEGY: "PRIVATIZATION OF PRIVATIZATION"

A timely and speedy privatization of Eastern European countries demands that the process be decentralized and that state control of the process be significantly lessened.

As a result of prior economic reforms, significant decentralization already exists, and many enterprises are operating under self-management principles. The use of a decentralized privatization strategy is particularly appropriate for such enterprises; otherwise it would be necessary to renationalize an enterprise in order to effectively privatize it through a centrally mandated mechanism.

The decentralized approach is particularly suited to attracting private and foreign investors, because these investors can directly enter into a joint venture or other transaction with Eastern European enterprises. These enterprises can also directly seek joint venture partners.

Methods/Techniques

There is no single privatization technique. Implementation requires a flexible approach employing different and varied approaches. Some effective techniques include:

1. *Spontaneous Privatization.* Spontaneous privatization emphasizes individual initiative or responsibility and permits an enterprise to organize its own privatization, whether in whole or in part. For example, a division or any part of an enterprise could be restructured to constitute a separate entity.
2. *Leveraged Buy Out (LBO).* The LBO approaches permit a privatized enterprise to finance the privatization from future earnings and avoid the time-consuming effort of raising the cost of an acquisition.
3. *Vouchers.* The vouchers approach, though controversial, should be tested. In Poland and Czechoslovakia there is already legis-

lation to implement such a system, and it will be very important to see how these work.

In the Czech system, vouchers would be distributed to Czech citizens, who would have the right to exchange them for shares in any enterprise, provided that no more than a minority interest can be so acquired. The exchange of vouchers for shares would be effected through an auction. The board of directors of an enterprise would have the right to sell remaining shares.

In the Polish system, any enterprise is transferred into a joint-stock company that is owned 100 percent by the state. A minority share of 30 percent is transferred to persons possessing vouchers. The company is valued prior to the transfer by a government agency and the vouchers are assigned a price. The vouchers are exchanged into shares through a subscription.

A small percentage of enterprises can be acquired by the existing employees at a reduced price. Investors, whether foreign or local, would acquire a significant share, and the balance would be retained by the state treasury as non-voting stock.

The formation of holding companies, though advancing commercialization of the economy, postpones privatization.

Because of West Germany's unique and broad financial support of East Germany, West Germany's privatization process is not an appropriate model for other Eastern European countries.

EVALUATION

Effective privatization requires independent advisers (including attorneys and management consultants), the existence of workable standard accounting and evaluation procedures, the employment of due diligence or review processes and mechanisms for rendering independent expert valuation, and other opinions on privatizing enterprises. It is very important that the regulatory process for privatization be conducted in an open and precedent-setting manner.

Legal and Regulatory Framework

Privatization requires the rapid creation of a commercial legal environment comparable to those in the countries of the European

Common Market. In particular, development of the following legal codes should receive priority:

1. commercial/corporate code;
2. security laws and regulations;
3. tax code;
4. antitrust or monopoly code; and
5. bankruptcy law and procedures.

All laws shall conform with European Community rules and regulations. In interpreting such codes, considerable, and perhaps persuasive, interpretative weight should be given to the decisions of courts and other applicable authorities.

Training and Expert Advice

Privatization will require extensive management training programs for enterprise employees and management as well as for government officials. Enterprises and government ministries should solicit and rely on independent, professional advice.

Information Service

A Standard & Poor's information service about enterprises and economic/market performance needs to be created.

SUMMARY

In the course of privatization, there are bound to be failures and disappointments, as well as growing unemployment and even corruption, such as stock manipulation. These setbacks should not be allowed to stop the privatization process or to deter the government and the people. Privatization is not a quick fix but a long-term process and solution.

APPENDIX 11-1: A CHECKLIST FOR PRIVATIZATION

Following is an issues checklist to be considered in the privatization of an economy.

A. Privatization
    a. Definition (what is it and what are its goals)
        i.   Complete ownership by non-state entities
        ii. Mixed private and state ownership
        iii. Differentiation in ownership according to industry or sector
            aa. utilities
            bb. other
    b. Goals
        i.   Increased investment
        ii. Creation of a middle class through the establishment of small and medium-sized companies
        iii. Reduction of the state sector
        iv. Other
B. Basic Issues
    a. General
        i.   Speed
        ii. Fairness, equity, or justice
        iii. Preference
            aa. enterprise employees
            bb. management
            cc. industrial-sector employees
            dd. other
        iv. Foreign investors
            aa. sell-out
            bb. restrictions
                1. special restriction on land, real estate and use
                2. minimum investment
        v.   Original or former owners
            aa. restrictions on land use
            bb. payment for improved or increased value
            cc. cash settlement

          dd. rights of existing users

      vi.   Attraction of new or additional capital and technology

      vii. Break-up of monopolies

      viii. Spontaneous privatization—the "privatization of privatization" (that is, less government intervention or participation in the privatization process, other than the enactment of enabling legislation and the creation of appropriate investment and business climate)

  b. Special

      i.   Social net

         aa. protection of existing employees (that is, job security)

         bb. unemployment payments

         cc. special and restricted cost-of-living payments for the public at large or certain identified groups—for example, senior citizens

      ii. Enterprise debt cancellation

      iii. Special government credits, allocations, and tax concessions

C. Methods of Privatizing

  a. Existing enterprises and service establishments (small, medium, and large)

      i.   Direct sale (negotiated)

         aa. lease

      ii. Auction

      iii. Employee stock ownership plan (ESOP) model

      iv. Cross ownership

      v.   Social dividend model

         aa. distribution of a basket of stock to each citizen

         bb. voucher system (together with auction or other transfer system)

  b. New enterprises

      i.   Entrepreneurial model (creation of new partnerships, cooperatives, and small private firms, establishment of new ventures in existing enterprises)

  c. Return of property to original owners

      i.   Conditions—for example, new investment

D. Financing Privatization
    a. Private capital
    b. Government credit
    c. Bank or institutional credit
    d. Tax credits or holidays
    e. Stock issuance
E. Specific Models
    a. East German *Treuhand*
    b. Alaskan Eskimo Trust
        i. Restricted sale for a period of time
        ii. Specified class as owners
F. Legal Framework
    a. Corporation law
        i. Civil law
            aa. German
            bb. European Economic Community
        ii. Common law
            aa. United Kingdom
            bb. United States
    b. Securities law
        i. European vs. U.S.
            aa. disclosure
            bb. registration
            cc. reports and prospectuses
            dd. restrictions on transfer sales
                1. insiders
                2. minimum holding period
    c. Land and property law
        i. Protection of private property
        ii. Rights of former owners
    d. Labor laws
        i. Right to hire and fire
        ii. Wages
        iii. Foreign workers
    e. Monopoly or antitrust legislation
    f. Special restrictions or obligations
        i. Requirements to "go public" after a period of time
        ii. Puts and calls
        iii. Other "venture capital"–type concepts

G. Negotiators and Advisers for the Privatizing Entity
   a. Negotiators
      i.   Existing management
      ii. Government employees specially authorized
      iii. Independent advisers or managers
   b. Advisers (independent)
      i.   Accountants
      ii. Lawyers
      iii. Consultants, including business and financial
      iv. Temporary managers
   c. Who pays
H. Potential Purchasers
   a. Foreigners
   b. Employees of an enterprise
   c. Management
   d. All citizens or residents
   e. The state
I. Capital Markets
   a. Types of securities
      i.   Stock
           aa. voting
           bb. non-voting
      ii. Bonds
      iii. Other debt
   b. Regulatory framework
      i.   Law
      ii. Regulatory institutions—for example, the U.S.
           Securities and Exchange Commission
   c. Trading framework
      i.   Stock exchanges
J. Recommendations/Plan of Action

12

Working Group 3:
Creating Capital Markets

Josef C. Brada

The creation of capital markets in Eastern Europe is important for two reasons. First, if industrial property is privatized, then such privatization is only meaningful if there are functioning capital markets to value this property and to facilitate its transfer from one person to another. Second, capital markets direct capital toward sectors of high return and increase efficiency by imposing financial discipline on firms.

We recommend enactment of a securities law that reflects the experience of developed market economies and that is broadly consistent with the practices of the European Community and the creation of securities-market institutions.

A key institution would be a government regulatory agency or commission, headed by appointed commissioners, to oversee the implementation of the securities law. Some members believed such commissioners should be appointed for terms that would ensure their independence, along the lines of the governors of the U.S. Federal Reserve System. Others believed that commissioners should serve at the pleasure of the prime minister or some other government authority. The commission would adopt rules for the functioning of securities markets and organize and discipline market participants until they were able to develop their own self-regulatory measures.

Everyone in the securities market—buyers and sellers as well as those providing investment advice—should be organized in an association open to all qualified persons. In some countries, a single location may be sufficient for a national exchange. In other countries, several locations may be required. The same rules should be followed in all locations, and there should be a central registry of shareowners.

The association would establish eligibility criteria for brokers, license market participants, and set standards of conduct and rules for the operation of the securities market, including the provision of information regarding the trading activity of members.

Some group members believed that this association should also operate the exchange or exchanges. Other members of the working group believed that the exchange itself should be organized and operated by the government, possibly through a quasi-public corporation. The former solution is more in keeping with U.S. practice and represents an evolutionary, and, arguably, more market-oriented, approach. The history of financial innovations also suggests that market-driven innovations and regulations are more successful than government ones. On the other hand, the exchange can be viewed as a quasi-public good, within the government's legitimate scope.

Moreover, the government may be able to finance the initial expenses of creating the exchange better than a fee-financed association. Hungary and Poland have opted for this approach. The association will have the right to monitor, and, if necessary, discipline members. Association actions shall be subject to oversight by, and appeal to, the commission.

The commission shall determine the record-keeping, reporting, and capital requirements for dealers. The commission shall also determine the information that issuers of securities must provide, both at the time of the initial offer and subsequently on a periodic basis. The commission will also determine to whom the information must be disseminated. These provisions will not apply to government or central bank issues or guaranteed securities, various forms of trade and short-term debt, and stock of small or narrowly held corporations. Sale of securities would be permitted only if this information were available to buyers.

The commission would also require the filing of information from individuals soliciting proxies or who are attempting to acquire more than some set percentage of a firm's outstanding voting stock. Also falling within the commission's reporting requirements are tender offers. Rules governing tender offers should provide for equitable treatment of all shareholders.

The law should also provide for the establishment and regulation of mutual funds. At first these should be open-ended for buyers but close-ended for sellers, because markets may be thin, making redemption expensive for the fund. As the market develops, redemption at net asset value should become possible. Some members believed that efforts to legislate financial innovation are not useful. The design of financial instruments, as well as limitations on the evolution of such features as futures contracts and warrants, should be determined by the market demand for these instruments.

There should be clear definitions of, and prohibitions against, undesirable activities, such as insider trading and churning, as well as regulation of borrowing for the purchase of stock.

Clearing transactions and recording ownership will take place through a national system. Fees charged for those services would accrue to the exchange if it were privately owned, and to the government if it owned the exchange.

As designed, such a stock exchange may be overdeveloped given the small number of privatized firms and tradeable shares. Nevertheless, a large centralized system will be able to handle the expansion of private companies, provide a framework for the future growth of exchange activities, and take advantage of modern technology from the outset, which will forestall potentially high, future conversion costs.

Index

About the Contributors

DAVID B. AUDRETSCH is Research Fellow, Small Business Management Institute, Berlin.

ANDREW G. BERG is Adviser to the Polish Ministry of Ownership Changes, and Member, Steering Committee on Mass Privatization.

JOSEF C. BRADA is Professor of Economics, Arizona State University, and Editor, *Journal of Comparative Economics.*

OLDRICH DEDEK is Deputy Director, Institute of Economics, Czechoslovak Academy of Sciences.

DAVID P. ELLERMAN is Co-founder, GEA Ventures, a consulting firm specializing in restructuring and privatizing enterprises in Eastern Europe with significant manager/worker ownership.

GREGORY JEDRZEJCZAK is Adviser to the Minister of Finance, Ministry of Finance, Poland, and Associate Professor, School of Management, Warsaw University.

ROBERT L. KONSKI is Adviser to the Minister of Finance, Ministry of Finance, Poland.

MICHAL MEJSTRIK is Director of Research Projects and International Contacts, Institute of Economic Sciences, Charles University, Prague.

KALMAN MIZSEI is Director of Research, Institute for World Economics of the Hungarian Academy of Sciences.

TEA PETRIN is Professor of Economics, University of Lubljana.

JENIK RADON is Vice-Chairman, Polish-U.S. Economic Council, and Partner, Radon & Ishizumi.

CATHERINE M. SOKIL is Professor of Economics, Middlebury College.

ALES VAHCIC is Co-founder, GEA Ventures, a consulting firm specializing in restructuring and privatizing enterprises in Eastern Europe with significant manager/worker ownership.

HEATHER L. WAYLAND is Research Assistant, Small Business Management Institute, Berlin, and Student, Stanford University.

About the Editors

MICHAEL P. CLAUDON is President and Managing Director of the Geonomics Institute and Professor of Economics at Middlebury College, Middlebury, Vermont. He has published numerous articles and books and is co-editor of four other volumes in, and serves as series editor for, the Geonomics Institute for International Economic Advancement Series. Claudon is a frequent commentator on topics concerning the emerging economies of the Soviet Union and Eastern Europe.

TAMAR L. GUTNER is Research Director at the Geonomics Institute. Previously, as a financial reporter for A.P.–Dow Jones and as a freelance writer, she wrote extensively on issues of economic reform in Eastern Europe and on international trade, finance, and markets. She is the author of *The Story of SAIS*, a history of the Johns Hopkins University School of Advanced International Studies, where she obtained her M.A. in International Relations.

List of Seminar Participants

David B. Audretsch
Research Fellow
Small Business Management
  Institute
Berlin

Stuart Bensley
Manager of Corporate Business—
  Middle East
Brown & Root, Inc.

Michel C. Bergerac
Former Chairman of the Board,
  President, and CEO
Revlon, Inc.;
Former President
ITT Europe Inc.

Valdis Birkavs
Deputy
Latvian Parliament;
President
Jurists Association of Latvia;
Vice President
Association of Soviet Lawyers

Josef C. Brada
Professor of Economics
Arizona State University;
Editor
Journal of Comparative Economics

A. Lewis Burridge
Chairman
Edward Aycoth & Company, Inc.

Michael P. Claudon
President and Managing Director
Geonomics Institute

Istvan Csillag
Financial Research Corporation
Budapest

Oldrich Dedek
Deputy Director
Institute of Economics
Czechoslovak Academy of Sciences

David P. Ellerman
Co-founder
GEA Ventures
Yugoslavia

Dick Green
President
MMS International, Inc.

Zeke Hanzl
Deputy Commissioner
State of Vermont Economic
 Development Department

John Hardy
Director of Corporate
 Development and Finance
Brown & Root, Inc.

Jeremy Ingpen
Vice President
The Catalyst Group

George Jaeger
Director
Edward Aycoth & Company, Inc.

Gregory Jedrzejczak
Adviser to the Minister of Finance
Polish Ministry of Finance;
Associate Professor of Economics
Warsaw University

Peteris Jurjans
Attorney at Law

Thomas Kaligin
Founding Partner
Dr. Goutier, Dr. Kaligin, Knopf &
 Partner
Berlin

Robert Konski
Adviser to the Minister of Finance
Polish Ministry of Finance

Woodrow J. Kuhns
Political Analyst
United States Government

Franklin J. Lassman
Managing Director
QMS Eastern Hemisphere
 Operations

Michal Mejstrik
Director
Research Projects and
 International Contacts
Institute of Economic Sciences
Charles University
Prague

Kalman Mizsei
Director of Research
Institute for World Economics
Hungarian Academy of Sciences

Niko Pfund
Editor
New York University Press

Jenik Radon
Vice-Chairman
Polish-U.S. Economic Council;
Partner
Radon & Ishizumi

Peter Rona
Former President and CEO
IBJ Schroder Bank & Trust Co.

Christopher Rother
Founding Partner
Dr. Goutier, Dr. Kaligin, Knopf &
 Partner
Berlin

Catherine M. Sokil
Professor of Economics
Middlebury College

W. Paul Tippett
Former Chairman and CEO
American Motors Corporation

William J. Williams, Jr.
Partner
Sullivan & Cromwell

Katharine R. Wright
Vice President
Center for International
   Management Education, Inc.

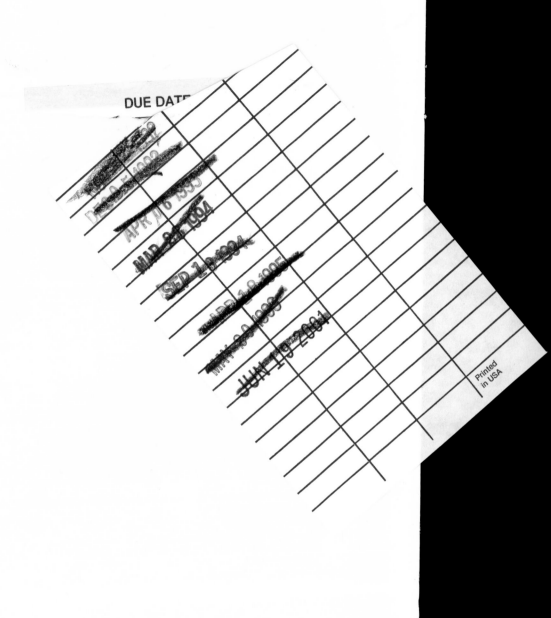

DUE DATE

APR 6 1993

SEP 1 8 1994

JUN 19 2001

Printed
in USA